NOAH'S ARK

Historical and Prophetic Truths

DON T. PHILLIPS

"Noah's Ark – Historical and Prophetic Proofs," by Don T. Phillips. ISBN 978-1-62137-950-8 (hardcover).

Published 2017 by Virtualbookworm.com Publishing Inc., P.O. Box 9949, College Station, TX 77845, US. ©2017 Don T. Phillips.

Table of Contents

Chapter 1

The Historical Setting

Noah's ark is known to almost everyone, whether they are Christians or nonbelievers. Children are told the story of how Noah was called by God to build a great ark in which he would place animals and fowl of every kind. The picture on the right is typical of what might be shown as the narrative unfolds. As we shall see, the stories which are often told are usually full of both factual errors and fantasies. As you read and study the complete and biblical record of Noah's ark, it will become apparent that there is more to this story than meets the casual eye. Before we begin our journey, see if you can spot at least five errors which might be evident in this picture.

The Origin of Mankind

The story of Noah and the ark which he built using God's instructions began about 1657 years before the flood took place. It began in the Garden of Eden which God had created for Adam and Eve. In the beginning God made the heavens and all of the earth according to his good pleasure. He then made Adam and Eve to live in the garden, and they were to have dominion over all of the creatures which God had made. The story of Adam and Eve is probably just as well known as the story of Noah and the ark. Adam and Eve were created by God to commune with Him, and they walked together in the cool of the evening and talked with each other. Nothing was withheld from Adam and Eve: God gave them only one law to follow, and that was to never eat of the fruit which grew on the Tree of Knowledge of good and evil. Adam and Eve were created in innocence, without any sin upon them. In fact, they had no knowledge of sin or its consequences since they were not aware of good or evil. Everything was good because it was perfect: There was no thought of anything being evil because Eden was created holy and good.

Although Adam and Eve were sinless, the Garden of Eden was not protected from sin. In the dateless past, there had been a great rebellion in heaven between Satan and God. The story of this conflict is found in Isaiah 14 and Ezekiel 28:12-14.

[12] *How art thou fallen from heaven, O Lucifer, son of the morning! how art thou cut down to the ground, which didst weaken the nations!*
[13] *For thou hast said in thine heart, I will ascend into heaven, I will exalt my throne above the stars of God: I will sit also upon the mount of the congregation, in the sides of the north:*
[14] *I will ascend above the heights of the clouds; I will be like the most High*   Isaiah 14:12-14

Thou wast perfect in thy ways from the day that thou wast created, till iniquity was found in thee.   Ezekiel 28:15

Lucifer fell because he became haughty and proud, and wanted to be worshipped like God. He wanted to be like God and *be like the most High*. When Jesus Christ was tempted by Satan in the wilderness, He replied: *Get thee behind me, Satan: for it is written, thou shall worship the Lord thy God, and him only shall thou serve* (Luke 4:8). Satan was kicked out of heaven, and incredibly he was followed by 1/3 of all the holy angels which God had created (Revelation 12). These angels now seek to torment mankind and persuade both man and woman to sin against God. They are called *demons*. Lucifer in Isaiah 14:12 is universally identified as referring to Satan. The word Lucifer only appears once in the King James Bible and that is in Isaiah 14:12. Lucifer is the Vulgate translation of the Hebrew word הֵילֵל. According to Strong's Concordance it means *shining one* or *light-bearer*.

Lucifer/Satan entered into the Garden of Eden with only one purpose: To cause both Adam and Eve to sin. Satan has never changed either his tactics or his purpose since he entered the Garden of Eden almost 6000 years ago. Satan is a liar and the father of lies. John 10:10 declares that Satan *comes only to steal* and *kill and destroy.* And so he approached Adam and Eve as a (then) beautiful serpent. According to the ancient Book of Jubilees, when Adam and Eve lived in the Garden he actually spoke to the animals, so it should be no surprise that the serpent spoke to him. Satan mocked God, and preyed upon the innocent logic of Eve.

[1] Now *the serpent was more subtle than any beast of the field which the LORD God had made. And he said unto the woman, Yea, hath God said, Ye shall not eat of every tree of the Garden*

3

[2] *And the woman said unto the serpent, We may eat of the fruit of the trees of the garden:*

[3] *But of the fruit of the tree which is in the midst of the garden, God hath said, Ye shall not eat of it, neither shall ye touch it, lest ye die.*

[4] *And the serpent said unto the woman, Ye shall not surely die:*

[5] *For God doth know that in the day ye eat thereof, then your eyes shall be opened, and ye shall be as gods, knowing good and evil.*

[6] *And when the woman saw that the tree was good for food, and that it was pleasant to the eyes, and a tree to be desired to make one wise, she took of the fruit thereof, and did eat, and gave also unto her husband with her; and he did eat*   Genesis 3:1-6

Lucifer approached Eve with two logical arguments: (1) God said that if Eve would eat of the fruit of the tree called the Knowledge of Good and Evil she would die: Lucifer said that she would not die. (2) Lucifer told Eve that she would be *a God.* So Eve believed Lucifer and ate of the fruit. A common misconception is that she ate an apple: There is no indication that an apple was the fruit. In fact, all we know that it was fruit. Whatever fruit was eaten it was *pleasant to the eye.* The next act of Eve was as destructive as the first. Eve gave the fruit to Adam and *he did eat.* Another misconception was that Eve sinned, and then enticed her husband to eat also. It is commonly believed that Eve sinned and then dragged Adam down with her. The biblical account does not support this conclusion. Obviously, Adam was there with Eve. He stood and watched as Eve was deceived. God made man to rule over his wife in the spirit of a respecter, comforter and protector. Adam failed on all three counts: He stood by and said nothing. Adam was just as much at fault as Eve was in believing Satan. One might argue that Eve was alone when she ate the fruit, and approached Adam later. Even if this was the way it happened, Adam was a man with free will and free choice. He could have still refused to eat the fruit and follow God's command. In either case, Adam made the fatal decision to sin against God and partake of the truth. The consequence of sin is death.

For the wages of sin is death; but the gift of God is eternal life through Jesus Christ our Lord   Romans 6:23

God told Adam and Eve that they would surely die if they ate the fruit, but they did not immediately die. *Is this a conflicting verse in the Edenic account*? Of course not. Adam and Eve was to eat of the *Tree of Life* in the Garden of Eden and live forever in a sinless garden. When they ate of the fruit, the consequences were swift and immediate. God gave them *skins* to cover their nakedness, and He then *cast them out* of the Garden of Eden. At that point, the mortal bodies of Adam and Eve *began* to die. The promise of eternal life in the Garden of Eden was gone, but not the opportunity of eternal life. 4000 years later Jesus Christ died on the Cross of Calvary, and offered eternal life to all those old testament saints who died looking to the appearance of a redeemer who would take away their sins, and to all New Testament saints who believed upon the name of Jesus Christ and also had their sins forgiven.

Adam and Eve entered into a world that now required them to labor by the *sweat of their brow*. Adam did indeed die just as God had said after living 930 years. These years are counted from the moment that Adam set foot outside the Garden of

Eden. The Book of Genesis has carefully traced the birth of sons to Adam and their progeny. The scriptural record is quite clear that Noah was born to Lamech 777 years after Adam and Eve were cast out of the Garden of Eden (Genesis 5:28). Noah was 600 years old when the flood came upon the earth (Genesis 7:6). The following table is a summary of Adam's lineage from Adam leaving the garden of Eden to the great flood.

Name	Lived (Yrs)	Had Son	At Age		AY YEAR Year Born	Biblical Reference
Adam	930	Seth	130	Creation Yr	1	Gen 5:3
Seth	912	Enosh	105		131	Gen 5:6
Enosh	905	Cainan	90	Methusalah	236	Gen 5:9
Cainan/Kenan	910	Mahalalel	70	Dies	326	Gen 5:12
Mahalalel	895	Jared	65	1657	396	Gen 5:15
Jared	962	Enoch	162	Creation	461	Gen 5:18
Enoch	365	Methuselah	65	Year of Flood	623	Gen 5:21
Methuselah	969	Lamech	187	1657	688	Gen 5:25
Lamech	777	Noah	182	Shem Birth	875	Gen 5:28
Noah-600 @ Flood	950	Shem	502	1559	1057	Gen 11:10
Shem-Gen 11:10-Lived 600 yrs	600	Arphaaxed	100	Arphaaxed Birth	1559	Gen 11:10
Arphaaxed-Born 2Yrs after flood	438	Salah	35	1659	1659	Gen 11:12
Selah	433	Eber	30	Abram Covenant	1694	Gen 11:14
Eber	464	Peleg	34	1729	1724	Gen 11:16
Peleg	239	Reu	30	Abram 75 when	1758	Gen 11:18
Reu	239	Serug	32	enters Canaan	1788	Gen 11:20
Serug	230	Nabor	30	2024	1820	Gen 11:22
Nahor	148	Terah	29	Terah died in	1850	Gen 11:24
Terah	205	Abraham	70	2084	1879	Gen 11:26
Abraham...75 entered Canaan	175	Isaac	100	Abram 100 when	1949	Gen 21:5
Isaac	180	Jacob & Esau	60	Issac born	2049	Gen 25:26
Jacob	147	Joseph	91	2049	2109	See Below
Joseph	110				2200	Gen 50:22

The exact year in which the flood occurred is universally agreed to be in Year 1656 or 1657 after Adam and Eve were cast out of the garden. The difference of 1 year occurs based upon how the 1st year out of the garden is counted. The 1st way is to designate the first year that Adam and Eve spent outside the garden as year *zero*. This is consistent with the birth of a new baby. The first year of a child's life is called year zero: a person is not age one until a full year has passed. In fact, a person is zero years old for 364 days, and remains one year old until the second year passes. The other way to mark time for Adam is to recognize that that the first year outside of the garden is just that.... Adam's first year. Hence, in the Table just shown the great flood occurred during the 1657 th year of Adam on earth, and not the 1656th year as is commonly reported. In reality, it makes little difference: It is simply a way to count elapsed time. Noah was still without any ambiguity 600 years old when the flood came upon the earth. Later, we will discuss how one might attempt to determine either the Julian year or the Gregorian (modern) year in which the flood occurred.

Finally, it is recorded that Adam lived 930 years before he died. Note that Noah was born in AY (Adam's year) 875. Hence, Noah was a contemporary of Noah for 55 years. During the last 30-35 years Adam would no doubt tell Noah about the wonders of the Garden of Eden, how he and Eve succumbed to Satan and sinned, and the consequences of sin.

During this period of time it is reasonable to believe that Adam not only sat with Noah and discussed these things, but he also likely told anyone that would listen to him. The question is:

Who hath believed our report? and to whom is the arm of the LORD revealed?   Isaiah 53:1

The Fate of Mankind

When Adam and Eve were driven from the Garden of Eden by God they were alone in a new world which had been cursed and functioned quite differently from the pristine, ideal land of Eden. The single act of rebellion and sin by both Adam and Eve had far reaching effects upon both the physical and spiritual man. Physically, mankind was condemned to death without the

7

renewing and sustaining powers of the Tree of Life. Adam lived to be 930 years old after he left the Garden of Eden. The average age that man lived has steadily decreased so that it is now rare that anyone lives past age 100. The steady decline of man's average death age is in no place more evident than the Old Testament. Seth who was the son of Adam, lived to be 912 years old;, his son Lamech lived 777 years; Shem lived 600 years. Many years later, Abraham lived 175 years. Because of modern medicine and other factors, the average age of a person today in the United States is about 79 years: The oldest person alive is thought to be 125 years old (2016).

Progressively, each generation lived shorter and shorter lives. Adam was the first human created and must have been perfect in every way. After Adam and Eve fell, the environment in which man lived changed, and so did the earth itself. In the Garden of Eden there was evidently a protective canopy which prevented ultraviolet rays from penetrating. It also appears that there was no rain, but a mist which nourished and provided water. This is based upon the conditions that existed just after Adam was created. There is no indication that anything changed while Adam and Eve lived in the Garden.

[5] *And every plant of the field before it was in the earth, and every herb of the field before it grew: for the LORD God had not caused it to rain upon the earth, and there was not a man to till the ground.*

[6] *But there went up a mist from the earth, and watered the whole face of the ground* Genesis 2:5-6

Biblical scholars are divided as to whether these conditions persisted only while Adam and Eve were in the Garden of Eden.

It is, however, certain that Adam became the first farmer, and that he was forced to grow food by the *sweat of his brow* in the midst *of thistles and thorns* (Genesis 3:17-18). The effect of seasons and atmospheric conditions now became a reality without the protection previously given in the Garden of Eden.

The fact that there was a mist upon the land before the fall is no scriptural proof to assert that no rain fell until Noah's flood. However, there is some biblical hints that the first rain that ever fell upon the entire earth was upon the roof of Noah's ark. The following is a list of reasons why rain may not have occurred until the great flood (Donald B. DeYoung from Don Stewart, https://www.blueletterbible.org/faq/don_stewart/don_stewart _738.cfm).

1.No mention is made of rain on the earth until the Flood (Gen. 7:4,12). The original earth and the Garden of Eden were watered by streams, rivers, and mist instead of by rain (Genesis 2:5,6,10). These sources may have been replenished from groundwater. Humidity and mist are still effective today in watering plants. Part of Adam's responsibility in the garden may have been to provide irrigation for the vegetation (Gen. 2:15).

2.The vapor canopy that may have existed prior to the Flood would have greatly affected climate. It could have ruled out rain showers. With a uniform temperature over the entire earth, there would not have been significant high and low pressure regions that produce storms today. From the moment the canopy collapsed, rain would then become an everyday experience.

3.The rainbow represents a special covenant or promise of protection from another worldwide flood. The rainbow's appearance to Noah may have been its first occurrence in the sky (Gen. 9:8-17). Typical raindrops of sufficient size to cause a rainbow require atmosphere instability. Prior to the Flood, weather conditions were probably very stable.

If the earth did not experience rain before the Flood, then Noah's ark-building must have appeared especially foolish to his critics. Likewise, the faith of Noah described in Hebrews 11:7 was especially strong. Noah was warned about things not seen, which is perhaps a further indication that rain was not part of humanity's early experience. Even with this accumulated evidence, a final authoritative answer to this question of pre-Flood rain is not known (Donald B. DeYoung, *Weather and The Bible*, Grand Rapids, Eerdmans, 1992, pp. 112,113).

9

The Evolution of Mankind

As children were born to Adam and Eve, the devastating effects of sin began to take their toll. The first two male children born to Adam and Eve were Cain and Abel (Genesis 4:1-2). If we examine the Biblical account of Cain and Abel, we see that on one special occasion they both offered sacrifices to God. Abel's sacrifice was pleasing to God, but Cain's was not. Even though they both offered something to God, their hearts were different. Cain's heart was wicked and evil. God warned Cain that sin would be *at his door* and that sin had a desire for him. It is often taught that the sacrifice of Abel pleased God because it involved sacrificial blood, and the sacrifice of Cain was from the field. But the sanctity of an animal blood sacrifice would not be institutionalized until Moses received the Law from God at Mt. Sinai. It was not the *nature* of Cain's sacrifice that pleased God, it was the *manner* in which it was given. No matter why Abel's sacrifice pleased God, God required a sincere offering. Abel's heart was faithful and true to God, and his sacrifice was excellent in God's eyes. This is borne out in what happened next: When Cain realized that God was not pleased with his sacrifice but accepted Abel's, his heart became wicked. He was angry and jealous of his brother and killed him out of envy. His haughty heart was forever revealed in his reply to God when God asked where was Abel …. *Am I my brother's keeper*? The answer was given by the Apostle John over 4000 years later:

If a man say, I love God, and hateth his brother, he is a liar: for he that loveth not his brother whom he hath seen, how can he love God whom he hath not seen?   I John 4:20

This is the first act of manslaughter ever recorded in the Holy Scriptures.

Things only went downhill from there: The generations of Adam became wickeder and wickeder as time passed. A very strange event is recorded in Genesis 6.

[1] *And it came to pass, when men began to multiply on the face of the earth, and daughters were born unto them,*
[2] *That the sons of God saw the daughters of men that they were fair; and they took them wives of all which they chose.*
[3] *And the LORD said, My spirit shall not always strive with man, for that he also is flesh: yet his days shall be an hundred and twenty years.*
[4] *There were giants in the earth in those days; and also after that, when the sons of God came in unto the daughters of men, and they bare children to them, the same became mighty men which were of old, men of renown*
Genesis 6:1-4

The wickedness and evil on the earth spread all the way to heaven. Some of the holy angels (Sons of God) decided to come upon the earth and have sexual relations with women (daughters of men). The offspring of this unnatural, incestuous relationship was a *race of giants* called *Nephilim*. According to ancient Hebrew writings and the Book of Enoch, they were mighty warriors over 7 feet tall with 6 fingers and 6 toes. Of course, like every other act of sin this rebellion against God was fueled by Satan and his demonic forces. Satan undoubtedly reasoned that if he could pollute and corrupt the ancestral line of Satan that there would be no human worthy to birth the promised Messiah. Because of this terrible sin, the angels which participated in this rebellion against God were dealt with decisively and completely. They were all cast into a place called *Tartarus* where they will remain until the end of the 1000 year millennial kingdom.

For if God spared not the angels that sinned, but cast them down to hell, and delivered them into chains of darkness, to be reserved unto judgment　　　II Peter 2:4

(The Greek word translated as *hell* in this passage is *Tartarus*, which is a subterranean compartment of incarceration: Phillips, *Life After Death*)　Finally, the Lord could stand no more.

[5]　*And GOD saw that the wickedness of man was great in the earth, and that every imagination of the thoughts of his heart was only evil continually.*
[6]　*And it repented the LORD that he had made man on the earth, and it grieved him at his heart.*
[7]　*And the LORD said, I will destroy man whom I have created from the face of the earth; both man, and beast, and the creeping thing, and the fowls of the air; for it repenteth me that I have made them*　　　Genesis 6:5-7

What a terrible judgment that God pronounced upon men! Man was mired in sinful thoughts and deeds *continually*. It *Repented* (grieved) the Lord that He had ever made man!! And the Lord said that He would destroy every man beast, fowl and animal that was upon the earth!!! Even in His righteous anger, we now see God manifesting grace.

But Noah found grace in the eyes of the LORD　　　Genesis 6:8

Chapter 2

Noah: A Man of God

The Old Testament is full of superheroes who are remembered
and revered by Jews and Christians alike. Abraham, Isaac and
Jacob; Joseph and Moses; King David and his son Solomon; and
the Old Testament prophets. One who is usually not mentioned
or revered is Noah....and *Noah found grace in the eyes of the
Lord.* Imagine the world in which Noah lived. *GOD saw that the
wickedness of man was great in the earth, and that every
imagination of the thoughts of his heart was only evil
continually.* It must have been a terrible existence for Noah who
was surrounded by sin and every iniquity that pleased man.
There were no other Godly people to which Noah could talk; no
local "church gatherings" or "bible study groups" where he
could find men of God worshipping and praying. Noah must
have been quite a man. He stood firm in his belief and refused
to disobey God. It is more than interesting that Noah raised his
three sons to fear and worship the one true God. Because of his
unwavering faith, his three sons found mercy and grace through
him. Not only his sons, but he obviously made it clear that if
they were to marry, he would not bless any woman who was
not God-fearing and righteous. We will shortly see that only
Noah, his three sons and their wives would be spared from
destruction of everything that moved upon the face of the
earth. In preparing this book, I have come to admire Noah as
much as I admire Daniel, Enoch and Joseph. Even Abraham,
Moses and King David committed grievous sins as recorded in
the holy scriptures. Was Noah without sin? No, of course not.

13

All have sinned and fallen short of the righteousness of God. It was not the absence of sin that saved Noah and his family, but like David he understood grace and he spoke to God daily in a state of contriteness and regret for what he might have done. The Apostle Paul was like Noah, arguably the most influential and important person who ever spread the gospel. But Paul grieved over the sin nature that was upon him.

[18] *For I know that in me (that is, in my flesh,) dwelleth no good thing: for to will is present with me; but how to perform that which is good I find not.*
[19] *For the good that I would I do not: but the evil which I would not, that I do*   Romans 7:18-19

Have you ever felt that your prayers were not answered and that God is not listening? Noah must have prayed for his kinsman and for all of those who surrounded him in a sea of sin; and for 120 years before the great flood he must have been grieved that no one was listening and that God did not hear his prayers. And yet, he lived each day in faith. Oh that we today would be like Noah.

[8] *We are troubled on every side, yet not distressed; we are perplexed, but not in despair;*
[9] *Persecuted, but not forsaken; cast down, but not destroyed;*
[10] *Always bearing about in the body the dying of the Lord Jesus, that the life also of Jesus might be made manifest in our body*   II Corinthians 4:8-10

Noah was a man who stood alone in a godless world. Because of his faith he found favor in God and he walked with God (spiritually). There is no question that he was laughed at, ridiculed and called an idiot for building the ark. It is hard to imagine how people, and even Noah's family, might have treated Noah. Imagine Noah telling his children that they needed to help him build the largest boat ever constructed before that time. *Why they would ask?* *To escape a great flood that would inundate the whole world,* he would reply. We can imagine their answer; *Are you insane?.* There is no way to understand what might have been going through Noah's mind but Noah must have had great *faith* in God's word. It is also reasonable to assume that God either gave Noah a great deal of money through some avenue, or Noah had a great deal of money himself. The amount of wood that was needed must have been enormous, and likely had to be purchased and delivered from a wide area. Noah was obviously not in love with possessing money, but rather loved what he could do with it to please God. As the wood began to arrive, it had to be planed, finished and cut to size. Although not stated in the holy record, God must have enabled Noah to construct a very detailed set of construction plans. After all, building a boat the size of the ark would have been very complicated and had never been done before.

Since the ark would have many animal passengers, the interior of the ark would need to have many rooms of varying size. Two points should be made: *First,* there would be large animals to house such as an elephant or a giraffe, but most species of animals are small size. It is also reasonable to assume that it was not necessary or even desirable to have full-grown animals. Even babies or young animals would preserve the species nicely. Skeptics and non-believers have been quick to point out that no boat of any size would be large enough to preserve all of the species on earth. However, it would not be necessary to load sea creatures or fish into the ark; they would do just fine. The

Bible makes it clear that the cargo was limited to land-dwelling, air-breathing vertebrate animals; corresponding to modern birds, mammals, and reptiles, as well as their extinct counterparts. *Second*, some species would not require every breed or kind. For example, only a few different dogs or cats would be needed, the wide variety that exists today have evolved naturally and through genetic breeding. Insects were probably not collected and housed on the Ark: They could survive a flood by floating on debris such as vegetation mats or large logs. Under conservative assumptions, there were probably no more than 16,000 land animals and birds on the ark (John Woodmorappe) and calculations have shown that the ark would still be about 20% empty. Although one can debate and challenge the ability of the ark to accommodate all species of animals and fowls, the issue simply does not exist for a biblical literalist. If God told Noah to build an ark and load it full of every species, the ark was perfectly built and configured for that task.

[11] *The earth also was corrupt before God, and the earth was filled with violence.*

[12] *And God looked upon the earth, and, behold, it was corrupt; for all flesh had corrupted his way upon the earth.*

[13] *And God said unto Noah, The end of all flesh is come before me; for the earth is filled with violence through them; and, behold, I will destroy them with the earth*
Genesis 6:11-13

Imagine what Noah must have thought when he heard God utter these words. *All* flesh had become so wicked that God would destroy them from the earth that he had created. Noah was probably very afraid for both he and his immediate family,

16

because he was well aware *that none are righteous, no not one.* He must have been relieved when he heard what God said next.

Make thee an ark...   Genesis 6:14

Construction of the Ark

It is likely that Noah was taken by surprise, particularly if it had never rained before. *What is an ark? What For?* Before these thoughts might be uttered by Noah, God gives him a set of very specific instructions.

[14] *Make thee an ark of gopher wood; rooms shalt thou make in the ark, and shalt pitch it within and without with pitch.*
[15] *And this is the fashion which thou shalt make it of: The length of the ark shall be three hundred cubits, the breadth of it fifty cubits, and the height of it thirty cubits.*
[16] *A window shalt thou make to the ark, and in a cubit shalt thou finish it above; and the door of the ark shalt thou set in the side thereof; with lower, second, and third stories shalt thou make it*   Genesis 6:14-16

(1) The ark is to be constructed of *gopher wood*. This is a very unique instruction to Noah. The term Gopher wood is used only once in the entire bible and that is in Genesis 6:14. Its exact meaning is completely unknown, but Noah obviously knew what it was and where it could be obtained. The NIV, New Living Translation and the New English Translation use the term " cypress wood". This is simply the refusal to render the earliest identification of "gopher wood' as just that. Cypress is far from the only guess made by translators. Other trees and plants

17

include pine, cedar, fir, ebony (Bockart), wicker (Geddes), juniper (Castellus), acacia (Religious Tract Society), boxwood, or slimed bulrushes (Dawson). Many scriptures in modern versions of the Holy Bile take serious liberty with the Holy Word as it was recorded in Hebrew. Let the reader beware.

(2) The length of the ark was to be 300 cubits; the width 50 cubits and the depth 30 cubits. The cubit was an ancient unit of measurement which was defined to be the forearm length as measured from the end of the middle finger to the bottom of the elbow. Obviously, this could vary from person to person and one group of people to another. This table gives some examples of how a cubit was measured in ancient civilizations.

Culture	Centimeters	Inches
Hebrew (Short)	44.5	17.5
Hebrew (Long)	51.8	20.4
Egyptian (Short)	44.7	17.6
Egyptian (Long)	52.3	20.6
Babylonian	50.3	19.8
Common	45.7	18

It is generally believed that a cubit was about 20 inches in the time of Noah. This would mean that the ark would be about 500 feet long, 83 feet wide and 50 feet deep. In comparison, a football field is 300 feet long and 160 feet wide. The ark was to be three stories with each story about 16 feet high. At this size, the ark would have the volume capacity of over 2 million cubic feet and could hold over 550 railroad stock cars.

(3) The ark was to have only one door in and the same one door out. Its position is unknown, but it would make

Size comparison between average sized, one-story home and Noah's Ark. Illustration from *The World that Perished*.

18

good sense to place it as an entry to the 1st or 2nd floor of the ark accessed by a ramp. The ark was also to have a *window* which was described as *in a cubit*. The original Hebrew text seems to indicate that there was a series of windows of one cubit high and wide which encircled the ark somewhere near the top.

(4) It is interesting that God sealed the ark from the rain with *pitch* both inside and out.

(5) The ark is to be built with *many rooms*. We will shortly learn that the ark must by its intended purpose have "many rooms". Noah and his family (8 people in all) would need rooms; animals would need rooms; birds and fowls of the air would need rooms and small animals would need rooms.

Skeptics of the biblical account have claimed that no boat could have been built at that time which would be large enough to transport all species of animals which were on the earth at that time. Three questions emerge: (1) *How large was the ark?* (2) *Could Noah possibly build the ark without modern equipment?* (3) *How many animals were put on the ark?*

How large was the ark?

We have already addressed that question with an answer motivated by Genesis 6:15. Was the ark the largest boat ever built? Certainly up to that point in time, it was the largest ever built. Wood is not nearly as sturdy and

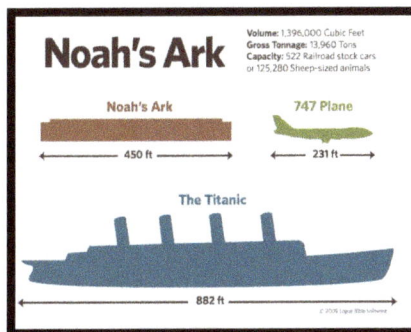

Noah's Ark

Volume: 1,396,000 Cubic Feet
Gross Tonnage: 13,960 Tons
Capacity: 522 Railroad stock cars or 125,280 Sheep-sized animals

Noah's Ark — 450 ft

747 Plane — 231 ft

The Titanic — 882 ft

strong as modern steel, and so several modern oceangoing vessels have been built which are larger in size. It can be assumed that the ark was the size that it was because God had a purpose for the Ark and He had Noah build the ark to do exactly what He intended for it to do. It is more than interesting that the ratio of length to width is 6:1, which is very desirable for stability. By any yardstick, the ark was huge. It had a capacity of over 500 railroad stock cars, enough to carry more than 120,000 medium-sized animals. So there was plenty of room on the Ark for the passengers, for their food and water, and for Noah and his family.

The Wrath of God

And, behold, I, even I, do bring a flood of waters upon the earth, to destroy all flesh, wherein is the breath of life, from under heaven; and everything that is in the earth shall die.
Genesis 6:17

God continues to speak with Noah, and reassures him that what is about to take place has never occurred before. Moreover, it is not an aberration of nature that will bring a great deluge of water upon the earth, but it is by God himself reflecting His omnipotence and unlimited power: It is *I, Even I.* The repetition of the personal pronoun *I* is to inform Noah that there is no higher power in heaven or on earth. The instrument of destruction is now fully revealed: It will be a flood of *water upon the earth.* This phrase has been endlessly debated and interpreted. Was the flood only upon the earth which surrounded the Mediterranean Sea, the Dead Sea and the Caspian sea, or should we stretch our mortal logic to include the whole world? There is really no debate at all for those who believe God's word. There is a popular bumper sticker that displays: *God said it, I believe it, and that is all there is to it.* I have news for whoever created and sold that phrase: If God said it...it makes no difference if you believe it or not...it is true. In Genesis 6:17 God tells Noah that He will *destroy all flesh* .....everything which has the breath of life and is under heaven. I do not know about anyone else, but this is a clear and direct statement that God intended to destroy all life upon the earth. This objective of the flood had previously been stated by God in Genesis 6:7, and it is repeated in Genesis 6:13 and Genesis 6:17

And the LORD said, I will destroy man whom I have created from the face of the earth; both man, and beast, and the creeping thing, and the fowls of the air; for it repenteth me that I have made them   Genesis 6:7

And God said unto Noah, The end of all flesh is come before me; for the earth is filled with violence through them; and, behold, I will destroy them with the earth.
                    Genesis 6:13

And, behold, I, even I, do bring a flood of waters upon the earth, to destroy all flesh, wherein is the breath of life, from under heaven; and everything that is in the earth shall die
                    Genesis 6:17

However, *where sin is made manifest, grace will abound*, and so we see in Genesis 6:8 the grace of God: *But Noah found Grace in the eyes of the Lord*. Because of the faith of Noah, not only did Noah find redemption and grace, but his wife, his sons and their wives (Genesis 7:1 ; Genesis 7:7). Since Noah and his wife sired their three sons, all of the men and women who will live and die upon the earth since the flood was actually from the seed of Noah. Unfortunately, Noah inherited the sin nature from Adam

21

and so everyone who ever lived would be born into sin. This is why Jesus Christ our Lord and Savior was conceived by God and called the *Son of God.* Since Jesus Christ lived a sinless life, He did not need to be redeemed by anyone....he was justified in Himself. This is the triumph of His sinless death on the Cross of Calvary.

Herein is love, not that we loved God, but that he loved us, and sent his Son to be the propitiation for our sins   I John 4:10

For he hath made him to be sin for us, who knew no sin; that we might be made the righteousness of God in him
        II Corinthians 5:21

Looking unto Jesus the author and finisher of our faith; who for the joy that was set before him endured the cross, despising the shame, and is set down at the right hand of the throne of God
        Hebrews 12:2

Fantasy or Fact ?

It has frequently been suggested that the flood was simply a literary story based upon another account of a great flood written sometime in the 2nd century BC, and that it was added to the Genesis account written by Moses in the 1st century BC. In the 19th century a team of archeologists digging

Epic of Gilgamesh Tablet

in Iraq uncovered a store of stone tablets near the Mesopotamian area of ancient Babylon. It was a story of how an ancient warrior named *Gilgamesh* undertook an epic journey to find the secrets of life and death. *Gilgamesh* was by legend King

22

of a mysterious kingdom called *Uruk*. The Epic of Gilgamesh is contained on twelve large tablets, and is believed to be one of the first literary classics ever composed. The tablets are ancient, and date back more than 2000 years before Christ. In his quest to find the secret of eternal life, he encounters a man named *Utnapishtim* who relates to Gilgamesh of how the gods told him to build a large boat to escape a devastating flood which inundated the earth and killed all mankind. Utnapishtim had become immortal after building a ship to weather the Great Deluge. He brought all of his relatives and all species of creatures aboard the vessel. Utnapishtim released birds to find land, and the ship landed upon a mountain after the flood. Even though many similarities exist between the two accounts, there still are serious differences (http://www.icr.org/article/noah-flood-gilgames).

Of course, to the Bible literalist there can be no doubt that the biblical account of Noah's flood is absolutely correct and proof of God's omnipotence.

The Purpose of the Ark

The ark was built by Noah at the command of God, and its purpose was to save Noah and his family from death and destruction. It was also constructed to save a remnant of the animal kingdom and the fowls which lived upon the earth prior to the flood.

And the LORD said unto Noah, Come thou and all thy house into the ark; for thee have I seen righteous before me in this generation   Genesis 7:1

[19] *And of every living thing of all flesh, two of every sort shalt thou bring into the ark, to keep them alive with thee; they shall be male and female.*

[20] *Of fowls after their kind, and of cattle after their kind, of every creeping thing of the earth after his of every sort shall come unto thee, to keep them alive.*

[21] *And take thou unto thee of all food that is eaten, and thou shalt gather it to thee; and it shall be for food for thee, and for them.*

[22] *Thus did Noah; according to all that God commanded him, so did he*   Genesis 6:17-2

[2] *Of every clean beast thou shalt take to thee by sevens, the male and his female: and of beasts that are not clean by two, the male and his female.*

[3] *Of fowls also of the air by sevens, the male and the female; to keep seed alive upon the face of all the earth.*
Genesis 7:2-3

[6] *And Noah was six hundred years old when the flood of waters was upon the earth.*

[7] *And Noah went in, and his sons, and his wife, and his sons' wives with him, into the ark, because of the waters of the flood.*

[8] *Of clean beasts, and of beasts that are not clean, and of fowls, and of everything that creepeth upon the earth,*

[9] *There went in two and two unto Noah into the ark, the male and the female, as God had commanded Noah*
Genesis 7:6-9

There has been countless songs, pictures and charactertures of Noah's Ark and it is commonly depicted as having two of each creature within the ark. Here we see that this is not true. There were actually *seven* of each clean animal and *two* of each unclean animal. The flood was almost 1000 years before when the law was given at Mt. Sinai and God restricted the Children of Israel from eating unclean animals. In Leviticus 11 and Deuteronomy 14 God told Moses and the people which animals, birds and fish were ritually unclean. The wording of Genesis 7:2 might indicate that there were to be seven clean males and females chosen and two unclean males and females loaded onto the ark. In any event, it is obvious that Noah was aware of which creatures were clean and unclean long before the law was given. It is interesting to understand that when Adam and Eve were cast out of the Garden of Eden, they were commanded to eat of the food which could be grown and harvested from the land. It was forbidden to eat meat or fish of any kind. After the flood, Noah and his offspring were told that they could eat clean animals, fish and fowl but no blood was to be consumed.

Noah was told that this was to keep the *seed alive*. Some have suggested that there were 7 pairs of clean animals so that Noah and his family would have food to eat. This is highly unlikely since the permission to eat meat/flesh was not given to man until *after* the flood. Noah had demonstrated that he had faith in the Lord, and his family believed also.

How long Did it Take to Build the Ark?

The length of time that Noah took to build the ark is not specifically given in the Holy Scriptures. However, there is a hint of how long it might have taken.

And the LORD said, My spirit shall not always strive with man, for that he also is flesh: yet his days shall be an hundred and twenty years. Genesis 6: 3

God had watched as man had become increasingly wicked and sinful, and His patience had run out. He spoke to Noah and told him that the death and destruction of all men was coming; only Noah, his 3 sons and their wives would be spared. God then stated that His *Spirit will not always strive with men*, and that *his days will be 120 years*. Genesis 6:3 is a difficult and hotly debated verse. There are two ways to interpret God's statement to Noah: (1) The Lord is prophesying to Noah and all the people that God's patience with the wickedness of man will come to an and after 120 more years; God will remove His spiritual protection at that time. (2) God is imposing a limitation on man that he would live no longer than 120 years of age. There are 2 verses relevant to Genesis 6:13.

And Noah begat three sons, Shem, Ham, and Japheth
Genesis 6:10

And Noah was six hundred years old when the flood of waters was upon the earth Genesis 7:6

From Genesis 5:32, we know that Noah was 500 years old when he began to have sons. From Genesis 7:6, the flood occurred in Noah's 600th year. Hence, the 120 year prophecy of Genesis 6:3 must have occurred 20 years before the 500th birthday of Noah. Genesis 6:10 does not necessarily chronologically follow Genesis 5:32. Many chapters of Genesis are not in chronological order (Genesis 1 and 2, for example). The purpose of Genesis 5 is to record a genealogical from Adam through Noah and his 3 sons. It would be awkward and unusual to interrupt a genealogical record with a prophecy of a great flood. There is no reason to not believe that the prophecy of Genesis 6:3 was not given 20 years before Noah was 500 years old.

The possibility that Genesis 6:3 was that God would limit the life span of any man or woman to 120 years is not supported by the scriptural records. Men and women continued to live longer than 120 years well after the flood. This fact is well documented in Genesis 11:10-26, Genesis 23:1, Genesis 25:7 and Genesis 47:28. Much later, Sarah lived to be 127 years (Gen. 23:1), Abraham lived to 175 years (Gen. 25:7) and Jacob lived 147 years before dying (Gen. 47:28).

The apostle Peter spoke of this in I Peter.

[18] *For Christ also hath once suffered for sins, the just for the unjust, that he might bring us to God, being put to death in the flesh, but quickened by the Spirit:*
[19] *By which also he went and preached unto the spirits in prison;*
[20] *Which sometime were disobedient, when once the longsuffering of God waited in the days of Noah, while the ark was a preparing, wherein few, that is, eight souls were saved by water*   I Peter 3:18-20

Both Genesis 6:3 and I Peter 3:20 are two witnesses that seem to confirm that God gave man in Noah's day 120 years to repent, or they would be destroyed. While it is not stated in the Holy scriptures, it would certainly be expected that from this time forward until the flood 120 years later, that Noah continually warned of the judgment to come.... but they ridiculed him and laughed at him. Just as today, salvation is by faith and is the individual choice of every person . This was once

27

again an act of pure *grace*. Of course, they would not listen and suffered the righteous wrath of God.

God's Covenant with Noah Before the Flood

[17] *And, behold, I, even I, do bring a flood of waters upon the earth, to destroy all flesh, wherein is the breath of life, from under heaven; and everything that is in the earth shall die.*
[18] *But with thee will I establish my* **covenant**; *and thou shalt come into the ark, thou, and thy sons, and thy wife, and thy sons' wives with thee* Genesis 6:17-18

God is true and merciful to those who remain faithful to His word. Those who reject God and His grace will reap what they sow. God announces to Noah that because of their sin and degradation that He will destroy all living mortal flesh from the face of the earth. His promise to Noah was that his wife, three sons and their wives will be spared from the Wrath of God. This is an *unconditional*, unilateral promise.

The 120 years of grace were over. God has warned His creation time and again that they were to love God with all of their hearts and to obey His commands. From the Biblical record, not one person responded to God's warning. The terrible fate which awaits them both in this life and in the life to come was now upon them. They had no one to blame but themselves as they all perished in sin.

Chapter 3

How Long Did the Flood Last?

The narrative of the flood in Genesis 6-8 gives rise to four interesting and interrelated questions: (1) *How long did it rain upon the ark?* (2) *How long was the ark upon the flood waters?* (3) *How long did Noah and his cargo of animals spend inside the ark?* and (4) *What calendar was used to record time before, during and after the flood?*

Noah Prepares for the Flood

In Genesis 6:3 God walked and spoke with Noah, as one man would talk to another (Genesis 6:9). He *lamented* that He had created man because of the wickedness and sin that filled the earth (Genesis 6:12). But *Noah found grace in the eyes of the Lord* (Genesis 6:8). Got spoke to Noah when he was 480 years old and told him that His spirit would be with the wicked men and women that He had created for only another 120 years (Genesis 6:3), and at the end of that time He would *destroy every man, beast and fowl* that He had created because it *lamented* (grieved) Him. However, *where sin abounds* much more does grace abound (Romans 5:20). God promised Noah that he, his sons and their wives (8 in all) .....along with a remnant of all animal and fowl species....would be saved from death and destruction. God then told Noah to *build an ark* which would serve as their refuge from the storm. Noah was 480 years old at the time and had a wife but no children (Genesis 5:32). We might pause to consider how remarkable that Noah was as both a husband and a father. Imagine Noah

29

going home that evening and telling his wife: *Woman, we have to sell everything we own to purchase wood to build an ark.* We can imagine his wife replying; *Are you insane! What is an ark?* Well, Noah would reply; *It is a boat...a very large boat.* It is well imagined that again she said: *You are insane! I can't even get you to build a grain storage bin. How are you going to buy all of this wood, build a gigantic boat, round up thousands of animals and birds and get them into this ark?* Noah would undoubtedly have scratched his head and said: *Don't know, but I do know one thing....God told me to do it and I am going to do it.* Oh what faith! Oh what an impossible task!! Oh what a man of God!!! It is recorded later that not one man in the entire world believed this "wild story" and stepped up to follow Noah...*not one.* so it is today....

[1] *Now the Spirit speaketh expressly, that in the latter times some shall depart from the faith, giving heed to seducing spirits, and doctrines of devils;*

[2] *Speaking lies in hypocrisy; having their conscience seared with a hot iron;*

[3] *Forbidding to marry, and commanding to abstain from meats, which God hath created to be received with thanksgiving of them which believe and know the truth*
Timothy 4:1-3

[37] *But as the days of Noah were, so shall also the coming of the Son of man be.*

[38] *For as in the days that were before the flood they were eating and drinking, marrying and giving in marriage, until the day that Noah entered into the ark,*

[39] *And knew not until the flood came, and took them all*

away; so shall also the coming of the Son of man be
    Matthew 24:37-39

The force of Matthew 24:38 is not to condemn man for eating, drinking and marrying but to warn of complacency.

[3] *Knowing this first, that there shall come in the last days*
    scoffers, walking after their own lusts,
[4] *And saying, Where is the promise of his coming? for since*
    the fathers fell asleep, all things continue as they were
    from the beginning of the creation.
[5] *For this they willingly are ignorant of, that by the word of*
    God the heavens were of old, and the earth standing out
    of the water and in the water:
[6] *Whereby the world that then was, being overflowed with*
    water, perished   II Peter 3:3-6

When Christ will suddenly appear in His 2nd coming, there are many who will "miss the boat". They will be more concerned with daily life and worldly pleasures than serving Jesus Christ in expectancy of His promised return.

God will always provide, and so at age 500 (20 years later) He visited Noah and his wife and in short time they were blessed with three sons; *Shem, Ham and Japheth* (Genesis 5:32). Here we once again realize what a great man and a great father was Noah. While not stated in the Holy Scriptures, it is not hard to imagine that Shem, Ham and Japheth experienced severe ridicule and social pressure as they grew up. We can imagine the taunting and whispers: *Here comes Shem, Ham and Japheth, those crazy sons of that nut, Noah.* Noah must have sat every evening with his sons and reassured them that there was only one sovereign God, and He was in control. We as parents could well learn from Noah how to raise our children today.

In complete submission to God Noah and his family labored on with perfect faith. Finally, after 120 years of preparation, labor and unwavering faith; things were done just as God had commanded. It is not hard to believe that God blessed Noah and his sons in many ways to finish the task set before them. I imagine they were never sick or tired; they were awarded with financial success to purchase supplies and raw materials; and they were comforted by God when the whole world rejected them.

Loading the Ark

How did Noah get all of the creatures into the ark? Skeptics and unbelievers say that Noah could not possibly round up all of those creatures...and they are right. The Bible clearly states that the animals *came to Noah* (Genesis 6:20); he did not have to round them all up. God apparently caused the animals to migrate to the ark and not resist loading, which took 7 days (Genesis 7:1-3). The Bible does not state how this was done, but it was done . We also do not know what the geography of the world was like before the flood. It is likely there was only one continent at that time, and if this is was the case then questions of how animals came to the ark from remote regions are not relevant. Keep in mind that this was a supernatural event which was orchestrated by God; no human could have done this.

[1] *And the LORD said unto Noah, Come thou and all thy house into the ark; for thee have I seen righteous before me in this generation.*

[2] *Of every clean beast thou shalt take to thee by sevens, the male and his female: and of beasts that are not clean by two, the male and his female.*
[3] *Of fowls also of the air by sevens, the male and the female; to keep seed alive upon the face of all the earth*
Genesis 7:1-3

They, and every beast after his kind, and all the cattle after their kind, and every creeping thing that creepeth upon the earth after his kind, and every fowl after his kind, every bird of every sort. Genesis 7:14

There is a common misconception that there were a pair of every animal, bird and fowl loaded into the ark. Genesis 7:2 reveals that there were 7 pair of clean beasts and 2 pair of unclean beasts, male and female. There is another misconception that there were 7 pair of every clean beast to provide food during the flood. The formal command to eat no unclean animal was not given until after the exodus from Egypt (Leviticus 11, Deuteronomy 14). The answer to this *mystery* is that after the flood was over and Noah left the ark, the first thing that he did was to build an alter to the Lord and offered up sacrifices to the Lord. The sacrifices were of *every clean animal and every clean bird* (Genesis 8:20). There were seven pairs of clean animals and birds to guarantee that sacrifices to the Lord would not eradicate the species. We are not told how Noah knew what how an animal or bird was unclean, but it is clear that he did know as he loaded the ark.

Noah had finished building the ark. He loaded it with *food* for him and his family, and food for all of the animals and fowls: The Lord then commanded him to load the animals and fowl.

Noah took 7 full days to accomplish this task. *After* 7 days, the rain came for 40 days and 40 nights.

[4] *For yet seven days, and I will cause it to rain upon the earth forty days and forty nights; and every living substance that I have made will I destroy from off the face of the earth.*

[10]   And it came to pass after seven days, that the waters of the flood were upon the earth.
Genesis 7:4,10

[7] *And Noah went in, and his sons, and his wife, and his sons' wives with him, into the ark, because of the waters of the flood.*

[8] *Of clean beasts, and of beasts that are not clean, and of fowls, and of everything that creepeth upon the earth,*

[9] *There went in two and two unto Noah into the ark, the male and the female, as God had commanded Noah*
Genesis 7:7-9

[5] *And Noah did according unto all that the LORD commanded him.*

[6] *And Noah was six hundred years old when the flood of waters was upon the earth*
Genesis 7:5-6

The Flood Begins

[11] *In the six hundredth year of Noah's life, in the second month, the seventeenth day of the month, the same day were all the fountains of the great deep broken up, and the windows of heaven were opened.*

[12] *And the rain was upon the earth forty days and forty nights*
Genesis 7:11-12

34

[17] *And the flood was forty days upon the earth; and the*
waters increased, and bare up the ark, and it was lift up
above the earth

[18] And the waters prevailed, and were increased greatly upon
the earth; and the ark went upon the face of the
waters.

[19] And the waters prevailed exceedingly upon the earth; and
all the high hills, that were under the whole heaven,
were covered.

[20] Fifteen cubits upward did the waters prevail; and the
mountains were covered.

Genesis 7:17-20

Here we have exact information concerning how long it rained upon all the earth. We are told in Genesis 7:11 exactly when the rain started to fall upon the ark. It was when Noah was 600 years old, on the 17th day of the 2nd month. Note that a deluge of rain fell for a full 40 days and 40 nights (Genesis 7:4,17). The rain was so heavy that the *windows of heaven* were opened.

However, this is not the only thing that caused the earth to be flooded. We are told that God caused all of the *fountains of the deep* to break open. This phrase is only found in Genesis 7:11 and Genesis 8:2. The subterranean earth is full of great aquifers of fresh

I will open the windows of heaven

water. God caused all of these aquifers called *fountains* to discharge their water upon the face of the earth. This would cause the surface topology to change: It was at this time that geologists believe the continents separated and the great oceans were formed. The waters increased upon the earth for *150 days* (Genesis 7-18, 7-24)

And the waters prevailed upon the earth an hundred and fifty days   Genesis 7:24

The deluge has often been called a local flood, only covering the land in the areas of the Mediterranean Sea and Mesopotamia. However, this is impossible. The biblical account of the flood verifies that the waters covered **all** the hills (mountains) that were upon the earth to a depth of 15 cubits, or about 22.5 feet of water (Genesis 7:19-20). If the Holy Bible says that this is what happened....It is what happened! A local flood could not completely inundate and cover all mountains and hills even in a limited area. Water will always seek its own level, and it would simply spread over the valleys and lowlands leaving higher elevations dry. This would be a great flood indeed, but it would not destroy all living people and creatures. Some would simply move to higher ground. The Bible clearly teaches that **all flesh** died...every man (Genesis 7:21, Genesis 9:1). The global extent of the Flood is referred to more than 30 times in Genesis 6-9 alone. Friends, one cannot pick-and-choose which parts of the Bible are true and which are false. The flood narrative was set to words by Moses under the inspiration of God, and the scriptures confirm beyond a reasonable doubt that the flood was not local to the Mediterranean Sea area but world-wide.

[3] *And the waters returned from off the earth continually: and* ***after the end*** *of the hundred and fifty days the waters were abated.*

[4] *And the ark rested in the seventh month, on the seventeenth day of the month, upon the mountains of Ararat*
                    Genesis 8:3-4

Although the words of God are true, they are not always easy to understand. In order to accurately determine the duration of the great flood, one must pay particular attention to the when each event began and ended.

Study to shew thyself approved unto God, a workman that needeth not to be ashamed, rightly dividing the word of truth
     II Timothy 2:15

The scriptures plainly tell us valuable information about the duration of the flood. It rained for 150 days. The rain started on the 17th day of the 2nd month (Genesis 7:11) and it ended on the 17th day of the 7th month (Genesis 8:4).

This one fact has caused an entire body of theology to evolve concerning the type of calendar that might have existed when the flood came upon the earth. This in turn has caused biblical scholars to state without any scientific investigation the nature of a calendar that must have been in use at this time. The fact that God had ordained and implemented through man some sort of calendar is beyond dispute when the flood narrative is carefully studied. The Book of Genesis repeatedly refers to months and days by number in the biblical account. The references are very specific as to month and day. *First*, it should be agreed that the inhabitants of the earth between Adam and Eve and the flood must have had some form of calendar that was set in place to determine seasons of the year. Adam and Eve were told that they would need to work the land, plant and grow their own food and harvest their own crops to survive. Recall that animals were forbidden to be killed and eaten until after the flood came, so the descendents of Adam and Eve consumed only vegetables and fruit. Any farmer or gardener will tell you that different crops must be planted and harvested at different times, each in their own season. What did God create to determine times and seasons?

The Mystery of the Flood Chronology

And God said, Let there be lights in the firmament of the heaven to divide the day from the night; and let them be for signs, and for seasons, and for days, and years Genesis 1:14

When God created the earth he also set into the heavens *lights*. These lights were emanating lights (the Sun and far away stars) and reflective lights (the moon and planets). In our galaxy the purpose of these lights are to *divide day from night*, and to set in place *seasons, days* and *years*. Many scientists have postulated that *if there really was a flood*, it must have changed the rotation of the earth and it tilted upon its axis, which created different times and seasons. This is just meaningless speculation: The bible clearly states that the sun and moon were to govern His ordained seasons, not some events which effected the earth. When God made the heavens and the earth in 6 days, He rested on the 7th day and sanctified it as a day of rest.

[1] *Thus the heavens and the earth were finished, and all the host of them.*
[2] *And on the seventh day God ended his work which he had made; and he rested on the* seventh *day from all his work which he had made.*
[3] *And God blessed the seventh day, and sanctified it: because that in it he had rested from all his work which God created and made* Genesis 2:1-3

About 1500 years later, God reinforced His command to Adam and Eve and institutionalized it as part of the Mosaic Law.

[8] *Remember the Sabbath day, to keep it holy.*
[9] *Six days shalt thou labour, and do all thy work:*
[10] *But the seventh day is the Sabbath of the LORD thy God: in*
       it thou shalt not do any work, thou, nor thy son, nor
       thy daughter, thy manservant, nor thy maidservant, nor
       thy cattle, nor thy stranger that is within thy gates:
[11] *For in six days the LORD made heaven and earth, the sea,*
       and all that in them is, and rested the seventh day:
       wherefore the LORD blessed the Sabbath day, and
       hallowed it   Exodus 29:8-1

Many biblical scholars have concluded using Genesis 7:11 and Genesis 8:4, that the sun, moon and stars before the flood were regulated to define a 12 month year with 30 days in each month, and that after the flood cosmic upheavals and changes in the earth's rotation and orbit redefined a year to be 365.2425 days and not 360 days. There is not one shred of evidence to support these "theories". However, the biblical record *does* clearly reveal that the rain began on the 17th day of the 2^{cd} month (Genesis 7:11) and that the ark *rested* in the 7th month on the 17th day upon Mt Ararat (Genesis 8:4) and that this period of time is 150 days (Genesis 8:3).

The undeniable fact is that between the 17th day of the 2^{cd} month and the 17th day of the 7th month *could be* 5 months of 30 days each. The subsequent conclusion which has

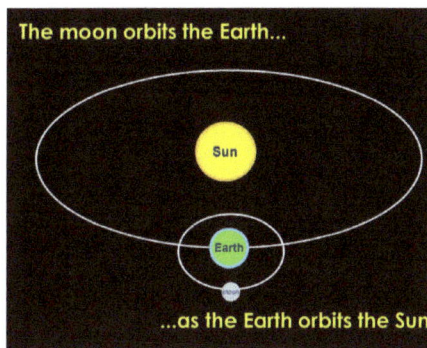

The moon orbits the Earth...

Sun

Earth

...as the Earth orbits the Sun

39

been reached was that the calendar in use at that time consisted of 12 months with 30 days in each month. This is taking a biblical fact and morphing it into a Biblical truth.

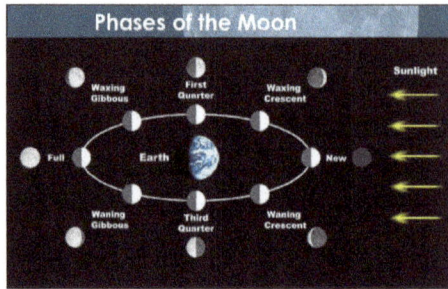
Phases of the Moon

For example, it is equally true that 3 months of 30 days, one month of 31 days and one month of 29 days will result in the same conclusion. The *extrapolation* continues: Since 5 months of 30 days apiece is **proposed** by many to *clearly* be the case, the sun, moon and stars were set in place to define 30 day months prior to the flood, and after the flood the pressures and effects of a world-wide flood were so great that the year changed to over 365 days. It is difficult to believe that the creative work of God was not sufficient to stand up to conditions that God in His omnipotence knew would come. It is more believable that just as God intended, the seasons, months and years have always been regulated and defined by the orbits of the earth, sun and moon. The earth is in a fixed orbit around the sun and the moon is in a fixed orbit around the earth. The earth completely turns at a slight tilt around an axis which runs from the north pole to the south pole in 23.93 hours; and this defines a day. As the earth rotates, it follows a fixed orbit around the sun, and it takes 365.242189 days (a tropical year) to make one complete orbit around the sun. As shown, the orbit of the earth about the sun is elliptical.

The tilt of the earth and the elliptical orbit both contribute to climatic conditions and the seasons. The poles are colder than the equator, and the seasons are caused by the fact that if the earth is closer to the sun, it is hotter and as the earth gets farther from the sun it is

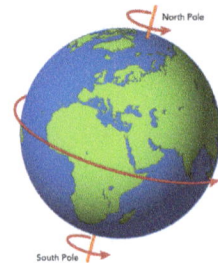

40

winter. These are overly simplified explanations, but are basically correct. The moon circles our earth and also follows a fixed orbit. The time that it takes the moon to complete one cycle around the earth is called a lunar cycle, and it takes is 29.530589 days (29 days, 12 hours 3.33 seconds). The rotation of the moon around the earth is remarkable: it is such that only one side of the moon (the same side) can be seen from the earth. The side that is seen is illuminated by the sun, and is in perpetual light, while the other side of the moon is in perpetual darkness. The purpose of this discussion is to emphasize and state that the week, days, months and years are defined by the earth, sun and moon from when they were put in place by God on the 4th day of creation. If God had changed this with the great flood He would have told us so.

And God said, Let there be lights in the firmament of the heaven to divide the day from the night; and let them be for signs, and for seasons, and for days, and years   Genesis 1:14

If our conjecture is true, and this author believes that it is, then how can one explain the fact that based upon Genesis 6-8 many scholars claim that a complete year at the time of the flood was 12 months of 30 days apiece; or 360 days in a year? We will show that this extrapolation and interpretation of God's word is completely false. The genesis account of the flood does establish that between the 2cd month, 17th day and the 7th month is 150 days. But the fact that the number of days between these two points in time is 150 days does not demand 5 months of 30 days apiece, or a 360 day year as many assume. In order to unravel this mystery and to find the truth of the biblical record requires a basic understanding of the Hebrew Calendar which has existed from ancient times. At first glance, the Hebrew calendar may appear very complicated, but some careful study will reveal that it is not. The Jewish rabbi Rambam

41

wrote that: "Basics of the calculated Hebrew calendar can be mastered by the average school child in 3-4 days" (Tractate Hilkhot Qiddush, HaHodesh 11.4

The Hebrew Calendar

The rules for constructing the Hebrew calendar were a closely guarded secret which was passed down through the centuries from one high priest to the next. In the 4th century BC, Hillel II published an entire set of rules for calculating the Hebrew/Jewish calendar. The Jewish calendar is what is called a lunar calendar because it follows the cycle of the moon and not that of the sun. The cycle of one new moon to the is almost exactly 29.5 days. The basic or normal Jewish calendar consists of 12 months, alternating between 29 and 30 days since a month of 29.5 days makes no sense. Simple math will yield a calendar year of 354 days. The modern Gregorian Calendar is used in most countries today. It is a solar calendar composed of 12 months. It normally contains one 28 day month, four 30 day months and seven 31 day months. This produces a year of 365 days. Since a solar year is about

354 Day Hebrew Year (*Normal year*)

Month	Number	Length	Gregorian Month
Tishri	1	30 Days	September/October
Chesvan	2	29 Days	October/November
Kislev	3	30 Days	November/December
Tevet	4	29 Days	December/January
Shebat	5	30 Days	January/February
Adar	6	29 Days	February/March
Nisan	7	30 Days	March/April
Iyyar	8	29 Days	April/May
Sivan	9	30 Days	May/June
Tammuz	10	29 Days	June/July
Av	11	30 Days	July/August
Elul	12	29 Days	August/September

365.2524 days, an extra day is added to the month of February every 4 years and another day is added every 100 years to a century that can be divided by 4. The Gregorian calendar is extremely accurate.

The difficulty of using a Lunar calendar is in three ways obvious: (1) The Solar calendar will accurately track the four seasons of Fall, Summer, Spring and Winter but the Lunar Jewish calendar will not. (2) Because the normal Jewish Lunar calendar is only 354 days long, it will fall short of tracking the Solar calendar by about 11.25 days every year. In other words, if both started on the same day of the year, after 3 years the Lunar calendar would lag about 34 days behind the Solar calendar. In about 18 years, the day of Christmas would fall in the month of July. About every 36 years, the two calendars would resynchronize but still be off by a fraction of a day. (3) The year that the Exodus took place from Egypt, God put into place Seven Feasts of Israel to commemorate the deliverance of the Children of Israel from Egyptian bondage, and placed them on the Jewish calendar as a perpetual memorial. Three were in the spring and three were in the fall. The feast of Pentecost fell in the Gregorian months of either May or June. If the basic 354 day Jewish calendar was to be used exclusively, The Feast days would rarely occur on the day and in the months that God had sanctified and placed them. This relationship of the lunar cycles to the solar year would create both agricultural and spiritual chaos.

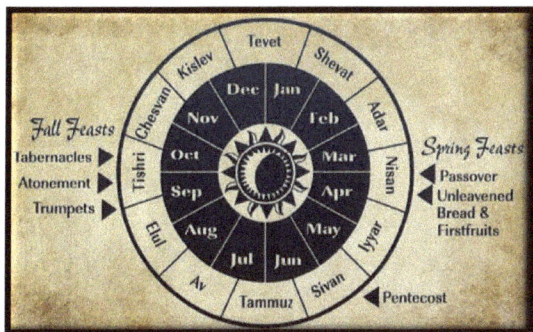

Note that as previously discussed, the generations of Adam and Eve all the way to the Noahidic flood were strictly an agricultural society since they were forbidden to

43

eat meat. Even after the flood when animals could be consumed (without the blood), the Jewish nation would raise sheep and doves for meals and sacrifices, but they were still dependent upon agricultural products as we are today. It is entirely believable that God was well aware of these problems from the moment that God cast Adam and Eve out of the Garden of Eden. It is not revealed to us in the Holy Scriptures, but it is highly likely and believable that God would reveal to Adam and Eve a way to synchronize a Hebrew Lunar calendar with the planting and reaping seasons of spring, fall , summer and winter as they appear in a solar year.

The first problem was that without a calculator or a computer, how was a lunar cycle of 29.5 days and a solar cycle of 365.25 days known to ancient man? There is a common belief, even by Jewish Rabbis, that the first day of each month was determined in ancient times by observation. As soon as the moon waxed dark, it would only be a matter of time until the first sliver of a new moon would appear. Two witnesses were required to report this occurrence to the High Priest and a new moon cycle was declared, which set the first day of each month in place. But what if weather conditions (clouds or rain) obscured the new moon? In this case, after 2 days the high priest would declare a new month and set it in place. But, how did the high priest know when to do this if it was cloudy, raining, overcast or foggy? Common logic would dictate that he already knew the length of each month was very near 29.5 days, and the sight of two witnesses was just a convenient way to begin each month and involve the people. How would the high priest possess this knowledge? It is clear that from the very beginning of time, even before there was a Levitical priesthood, that the duration of a lunar cycle could easily be determined by observation, as

44

could the length of a solar year. It would not take more that 40-50 years to not only determine an accurate lunar and solar cycle of time, but also recognize when the longest day (summer solstice) and the shortest day(winter solstice) of the year would occur. Do we doubt that this could not be accomplished? Consider other civilizations faced with the same problems. The ancient Maya built pyramids which accurately predicted the summer and winter solstice, and they even developed a calendar just as accurate as we have today! The famous Stonehenge ruins in England have been shown to function as a gigantic stone calendar for agricultural and spiritual purposes. The Egyptians built and aligned their great pyramids around heavenly bodies, and developed an elegant but simple calendar to predict when the Nile River would flood every year; all with hand calculations and visual observations. It is interesting to note that the Egyptian calendar consisted of 12 months with 30 days in each month, but they added 5 days to the 12th month each year making a 365 day calendar. This calendar was developed hundreds of years after the flood, and this will prove to be an important observation.

It is clear that Adam and Eve, Noah and his descendents, had to develop and maintain a 12 month calendar that would not only start each month with a new moon (full moon on the 14th or 15th day of each month), but would also accurately track the four seasons. This knowledge, as just discussed, would have to be known almost immediately. Various rules were likely developed or implemented by direct revelation and instructions from God to add days to certain months to help align the lunar calendar with the solar calendar. A major adjustment revealed by Hillel II when he published calendar rules was to add a 13th month of 30 days (Adar II) to the basic 12 month calendar 7 times every 19 years. These years were called *leap years*. Recall that about every 3 years the Lunar year would fall behind the solar year about one month. The Hebrew/Jewish years *before* a leap year would slowly *lose* days against a solar year. When a Leap year would occur, all dates following Adar II would be shoved *ahead* of Solar year dates and slowly drop back to a true solar date. This is why , for example, that every Hebrew/Jewish year is shown to occur in one of two Gregorian calendar months. For example, in 2016 Nisan 1 fell on April 9; in 2017 it will fall on March 26. Using several other adjustments, the Jewish Lunar calendar would coincide with the modern Gregorian Solar calendar every 19 years. This is called a *Metonic Cycle*. There are 7 Leap Years in a Metonic Cycle. Details of a Metonic cycle can be found in *The Comprehensive Hebrew Calendar* by Arthur Spier.

Finally, the modern Gregorian calendar was introduced in October of 1582 under Pope Gregory XII. The current Hebrew/Jewish calendar was made public by Hillel b. Yehuda (358-359 BC) after centuries of secrecy under the Levitical priesthood. If there was a calculated Hebrew calendar before the Exodus, it was a lot simpler than the rules that were used today. This is because there were special rules introduced after God instituted the Feasts of Israel following the Exodus in 1450 BC. The purpose of all this complicated discussion is to establish that any Hebrew/Jewish Lunar calendar must *always* synchronize the lunar calendar and the solar calendar in the same way. It is a simplification, but the modern rules try to keep two Sabbath days from falling back-to back and several other minor problems. This is accomplished by invoking what is called *rules of postponement.*

What Calendar Was in Use Before and After the Flood ?

Biblical scholars generally state without further investigation that the Hebrew calendar at the time of Noah's flood consisted of 12 months, with each month being 30 days in length. This is because comparing Genesis 7: 11&24 to Genesis 8: 3&4 in the biblical account of the flood, 150 days passed between the 17th day of the 2cd month and the 17th day of the 7th month. On the surface, this seems to be conclusive proof... but is it? First, if this was true, it would be necessary to add 5 days at the end of every year to "synchronize" the lunar and solar year dates. One should note that even if this was done (as the Egyptians did much later) the 365th day per year calendar would still lose about 0.25 days per year against the 365.2425 day solar year. This may not seem to be much difference, but every 4 days the Lunar calendar of 365 days per year would lose 1 day against the 365.25 day solar year. Every 120 years, it would lose a whole 30 day month! It is easy to understand that this would be unacceptable.

We should also realize that one must be very careful to determine the time which can elapse between two points in time. Consider the time between Day 1 and Day 5 in the following sequence of days, with the first day beginning at 6:00 PM and the 5th day ending at 6:00 PM (New Jewish days begin at 6:00 PM and not at midnight)

Day 1	Day 2	Day 3	Day 4	Day 5
1	2	3	4	5

A casual and common answer would be (5-1)=4 days .If the 1st and 5th day are not counted inclusively, the answer is 3 days. If the question is answered by including days elapsed between

47

when the 1st day started and the 5th day ends, it is 5 days. So which is it? One must know the rules that will apply. We will let the Holy record dictate how to count the days between recorded events as we reconstruct the flood narrative.

[11] *In the six hundredth year of Noah's life, in the second month, the seventeenth day of the month,* **the same day** *were all the fountains of the great deep broken up, and the windows of heaven were opened.*

[24] *And the waters prevailed upon the earth an hundred and fifty days.*   Genesis 7:11, 24

[3] *And the waters returned from off the earth continually: and* **after the end** *of the hundred and fifty days the waters were abated.*

[4] *And the ark rested in the seventh month, on the seventeenth day of the month, upon the mountains of Ararat*   Genesis 8:3-4

According to Genesis 7:11, the rain began to fall on the 17th day of the 2cd month; *on the same day.* Genesis 8:3 states that *the waters prevailed* for 150 days; *after the end* of these 150 days, the waters *abated*. The Hebrew word for *abated* is *Chacer*. It is only used one time in the Old Testament and it is in Genesis 8:3. It means to decrease, fall or to make lower. This corresponds to the ark *resting* on the 17th day of the 7th month (Genesis 8:4). Multiple biblical scholars point to these verses and boldly declare: " Exactly 5 months of 30 days elapsed between the 17th day of the 2nd month and the 17th day of the 7th month. Hence, the calendar in use at that time was a 12 month calendar with

48

360 days in a year". These same scholars then really go out on a limb and explain that after the flood the orbit and tilt of the earth changed and the solar year shifted from 360 days to 365.2425 days as it is today. This all started with the observation that between the 17th day of the 2nd month and the 17th day of the 7th month *exactly* 150 days elapse. Does the biblical record support this conclusion? The answer is, NO.

The following graphic illustrates the first 7 months of a 12 month calendar using 30-day months. Days are numbered starting on the 17th day of the 2nd month.

Mo.	1	2	3	4	5	6	7	8	9	10	11	12	13	14	15	16	17	18	19	20	21	22	23	24	25	26	27	28	29	30
1																														
2																	1	2	3	4	5	6	7	8	9	10	11	12	13	14
3	15	16	17	18	19	20	21	22	23	24	25	26	27	28	29	30	31	32	33	34	35	36	37	38	39	40	41	42	43	44
4	45	46	47	48	49	50	51	52	53	54	55	56	57	58	59	60	61	62	63	64	65	66	67	68	69	70	71	72	73	74
5	75	76	77	78	79	80	81	82	83	84	85	86	87	88	89	90	91	92	93	94	95	96	97	98	99	100	101	102	103	104
6	105	106	107	108	109	110	111	112	113	114	115	116	117	118	119	120	121	122	123	124	125	126	127	128	129	130	131	132	133	134
7	135	136	137	138	139	140	141	142	143	144	145	146	147	148	149	150	151	152	153	154	155	156	157	158	159	160	161	162	163	164

On the surface, a duration of 150 days over a 5 month period starting on the 17th day of the 2nd month and ending on the 17th day of the 7th month seems to be a logical conclusion: But look again at the calendar that shows each day-count. *There is something wrong.* The Holy record clearly says that the flood rains began on *the 17th day of the 2nd month* (Gen 7:11), and the water was upon the earth (rained) for 150 days (Gen 7:24). Now note carefully that the waters abated (ceased to fall) on the 17th day of the 7th month *after the end of 150 days*. This is an *inclusive* count of 150 days, counting both Day1 and Day 150. To summarize, beginning on the 17th day of month 2 (Genesis 7:11), we count off 150 days (Genesis 8:3). But, the 150th day is on the **16th day** of month 7; *not* on the 17th day of month 7. The biblical record demands that the rains fell for 150 days including the first and the last day. *Further*, the 7th month could be any

49

length. Using 30 day months, the 17th day of the 7th month is actually 151 days after the rains started. It is also ridiculously stated by many biblical scholars that if the 1st four months are of 30 days duration, then *all* months must be 30 days apiece. They justify this conclusion by the Revelation record of John and not on the Genesis record.

Authors Note: The rejection of a 12 month year with 30 days in each month based upon the Genesis account also destroys the assumption that has been made by many prophecy teachers that a *prophetic year* in the bible is a 360 day year. Using this assumption, Sir Robert Anderson developed a complex theory based upon Daniels 70th week, which predicted that Jesus Christ was born on a Thursday in 32 AD. Many have erroneously accepted this theory as fact. Phillips has shown that Anderson was clearly wrong, and that Christ died on Wednesday in 30 AD in his book *The Birth and Death of Christ*.

Once again, it is clearly shown from the above table that the 150th day does *not* end on the 17th day of the 7th month, but on the 16th day of the 7th month. This completely disproves the theory that before and during the flood a 12 month calendar using 30 days per month was in existence. As we have pointed out, even if 150 days *elapsed* over a 5 month period of time is no proof that each month contained 30 days. Nor is it any proof whatsoever that an entire 12 month year at that time was 360 days long (12 months of 30 days). What the Holy Scriptures *clearly say* is that 150 days *must* elapse between the 17th day, 2^{cd} month and the 17th day, 7th month, inclusive. *So*:

Was a version of the Hebrew/Jewish calendar in use today being used that synchronized the Lunar year with the solar year in existence at the time of the flood? Is it possible that it was in existence by instructions from God since Adam left the Garden of Eden? Is there any proof that this is true, or is it just another "wild speculation"? "Proof" is a strong word, but there is very strong evidence that this is true. If we could show beyond reasonable doubt that the Hebrew calendar was being used when the flood came upon the earth; mission accomplished.

It is necessary to change a 360 day yearly lunar calendar by periodically adding days to make the Lunar calendar keep up with a 365.25 day solar calendar. To accomplish this synchronization, a set of months can be established which periodically add an extra day and an extra month over a 19 year period of time. Leap years are those years where it is necessary to add a whole month (Adar II) of 30 days.

The Hebrew calendar in use today balances the solar year with the lunar year. This means that it has been designed to never lag behind or get ahead of a solar calendar based upon a 365.25 day year. Each month is always either 29 or 30 days long to average to 29.5 days; which is the duration of one lunar month. A Hebrew calendar year is *regular* in that it will always have either 354, 355, or 366 days during a normal 12 month year; or 383, 384 or 385 years in a 13 month leap year. Because the Hebrew lunar months consist of 29 and 30 days, it is obvious that a solar year of 365.25 days can never be equal to any Hebrew year. Any Hebrew calendar year of 12 months will always "fall behind" a solar based calendar of 365 years. Hence, to "catch up" a 13 month year is periodically added (7 times in a 19 year cycle).

384 Day (Leap Year)

Tishrei · Heshvan · Kislev · Tevet · Shevat · Adar I · Adar II · Nisan · Iyyar · Sivan · Tammuz · Av · Elul

385 Day (Leap Year)

Tishrei · Heshvan · Kislev · Tevet · Shevat · Adar I · Adar II · Nisan · Iyyar · Sivan · Tammuz · Av · Elul

355 Day

Tishrei · Heshvan · Kislev · Tevet · Shevat · Adar I · Nisan · Iyyar · Sivan · Tammuz · Av · Elul

383 Day (Leap Year)

Tishrei · Heshvan · Kislev · Tevet · Shevat · Adar I · Adar II · Nisan · Iyyar · Sivan · Tammuz · Av · Elul

353 Day

Tishrei · Heshvan · Kislev · Tevet · Shevat · Adar I · Nisan · Iyyar · Sivan · Tammuz · Av · Elul

354 Day

Tishrei · Heshvan · Kislev · Tevet · Shevat · Adar I · Nisan · Iyyar · Sivan · Tammuz · Av · Elul

This set of months and years are uniquely combined over a period of 19 years such that on the first day of a 19 year cycle the solar and lunar calendar are exactly in sync. This pattern of months are repeated perpetually.

As shown, the Hebrew calendar has either 12 months of 353, 354 and 355 days or 13 months in which the extra month is either 383, 384 and 385 days. *A Hebrew/Jewish lunar calendar which tracks the solar year is **always one of the above years**. Is there a year in this set of 6 different Hebrew Calendar years that will contain 150 days between the 2nd month, 17th day and the 7th month, 17th day?* According to the Biblical account, the 17th day in both the 2nd and 7th month must be counted as we have previously shown from scripture. *Remarkably*, there is *one* and *only one* year that meets this requirement, and it is the 385 day leap year shown above. Do not get lost in this difficult discussion. We have shown that the year in which the Flood of Noah took place could have only been a 385 day Leap Year. To the best of this author's knowledge, *this is the only known calendar that currently exists or has existed through recorded time that meets this requirement*. If this is true, then there is strong evidence that God taught Adam and his descendents how to use the modern Hebrew calendar and it was in use at the time of the flood. The first 7 months of a 385 day Hebrew (leap) year are as follows.

Mo.	1	2	3	4	5	6	7	8	9	10	11	12	13	14	15	16	17	18	19	20	21	22	23	24	25	26	27	28	29	30	Days	Days	Mo. Name
1																															30		Tishri
2										1	2	3	4	5	6	7	1	2	3	4	5	6	7	8	9	10	11	12	13	14	30	14	Heshvan
3	15	16	17	18	19	20	21	22	23	24	25	26	27	28	29	30	31	32	33	34	35	36	37	38	39	40	41	42	43	44	30	44	Kislev
4	45	46	47	48	49	50	51	52	53	54	55	56	57	58	59	60	61	62	63	64	65	66	67	68	69	70	71	72	73		29	73	Tevet
5	74	75	76	77	78	79	80	81	82	83	84	85	86	87	88	89	90	91	92	93	94	95	96	97	98	99	100	101	102	103	30	103	Shevat
6	104	105	106	107	108	109	110	111	112	113	114	115	116	117	118	119	120	121	122	123	124	125	126	127	128	129	130	131	132	133	30	133	Adar I
7	134	135	136	137	138	139	140	141	142	143	144	145	146	147	148	149	150														29	150	Aar II

The 150 day period between Heshvan 17 (2nd month, 17th day) and Adar II (7th month, 17th day) start and end *exactly* as demanded by the Genesis account, and this is the only year in any known calendar which satisfies the Biblical account of the flood (KJV). The skeptical reader can count each of the days between Month 2, day 17 and Month 7, day 17 for each of the six different types of years, and verify this fact. In the 385 day Leap year shown above, above, the number of days between the Hebrew months Heshvan 17 and Adar II 17 is exactly (14+30+29+30+30+17)=150 days using inclusive reckoning as mandated by the Genesis account.

This remarkable result has been suggested previously by a Biblical Scholar named Don Roth. However, his analysis is different from that presented here. The main difference is when the 1st month of the year actually started in Noah's day.

Don Roth was convinced that the calendar in use at the time of the flood started in the month of *Nisan* and not the month of Tishri. It is believed that this cannot be true, and that the first month of the Jewish year before the exodus from Egypt occurred in 1490 BC was Tishri. The reason that this conclusion is thought to be true is that at the time of the exodus the children of Israel were redeemed from slavery following the death of every firstborn in Egypt *except* in those houses that the blood of a firstborn lamb was painted over the lintel of the door. The *death angel* came at Midnight in the evening of Nisan 14 (actually Nisan 15), after the Passover lamb that protected the Children of Israel was slain the afternoon of Nisan 14. To commemorate and institutionalize this great event, God declared Nisan 14 to be the Passover Feast and the evening of

Nisan 15 to be the first day of the Feast of Unleavened Bread. God gave the following commands to Israel.

And this day shall be unto you for a memorial; and ye shall keep it a feast to the LORD throughout your generations; ye shall keep it a feast by an ordinance forever Genesis 12:14

This month shall be unto you the beginning of months: it shall be the first month of the year to you Genesis 12:2

Careful study of the Genesis account will verify that *this day* is Nisan 14, and it is called the Jewish Feast of Passover. Note that God commanded Israel to designate the first month of the year as *Nisan*. Why would God issue this command if Nisan was already the first month of the year? The answer is, He *would not* unless Tishri was and had been the first month of the year forever up until that time. Note that God did not change anything about the Jewish calendar at all: All God did was to renumber the months. Incidentally, the Jewish calendar had no names for each month, only numbers, until the Babylonian exile almost 500 years later. This is why no month names were used in Genesis 7-9. In order to avoid confusion, Israel from that point on recognized two calendars; a *Civil calendar* with month 1 as *Tishri*.... and a *Religious calendar* with month 1 as *Nisan*: They continue that practice today. Again, if Tishri 1 was not the first day of the 1st month up until the exodus, there would be no need whatsoever to recognize a separate Civil and Religious year.

With this proved, we will answer the following questions: (1) *How long did the flood last* and (2) *How long was Noah, his family and the animals in the ark?*

55

The preceding discussion may have been difficult to follow, so let us recap what we have found. We were trying to prove that the Hebrew/Jewish calendar has been in use for a much longer time than previously thought: In particular; we postulate that it *could* have been in use at the time of Noah's flood. We have shown that he biblical account gives us the specific requirement that 150 days must exactly elapse between the beginning of the 2nd month, 17th day and the ending of the 7th month, 17th day, inclusive reckoning. A yearly calendar of 12 months each of 30 days *will not* satisfy this requirement, but a Hebrew calendar with a 385 day Leap year does *uniquely* match all biblical requirements.

It should be noted and conceded that an unadjusted yearly calendar with 12 months of 30 days each *would* satisfy the requirement to track a 29.5 day lunar cycle, but *could never* synchronize to the 365.25 day solar cycle. Such a calendar would be useless to predict the 4 seasons of spring, fall winter and summer. If the Hebrew/Jewish calendar *was* in use both before and during the flood of Noah it would do both. It is clear that *some* calendar was in use before and during the flood since the flood narrative meticulously documents the entire flood story by referencing both months and days corresponding to major events. In the previous analysis of the Hebrew/Jewish calendar we listed every possible year that will occur in a modern Hebrew calendar over a 19 year Metonic Cycle. The purpose of doing this was to determine if there was any type of year in the Hebrew/Jewish calendar that contained 150 days between the 2nd month, 17th day and the 7th month, 17th day. If there was not, than the Hebrew/Jewish calendar *could not* have been in use at the time of the flood. Remarkably, one and only one type of year passed the test: The 385 day leap year. This is an astonishing find, since no other known calendar in all of history has such a year. It is therefore concluded that the year of the flood was a 385 day year, and that a 360 day calendar year based upon the Genesis account taught should be rejected and abandoned.

So why is this such a "big deal"? If we are correct (and I think that we are), the Gregorian date (month and year) can be determined for the flood, the exodus, the date that Solomon's Temple was built and other biblical events. *How can this be done?* First, the lunar cycle of new moon to new moon (29.5 days) has existed since time began, and it has never changed. Neither has one solar cycle of 365.2524 days. Computer programs are now available to retrace time from any new moon today back thousands of years and equate that to the Gregorian solar based calendar in use today (I recommend a Hebrew to Gregorian Calendar program called *Abdicate* at *http://www.abdicate.net/*

The Flood Chronology

As we have shown, one must be very careful in using the Biblical narrative of the flood to determine when everything happened. We will do this one verse at a time. The following graphic will be used to determine when the flood began and ended, and also

Mo.	1	2	3	4	5	6	7	8	9	10	11	12	13	14	15	16	17	18	19	20	21	22	23	24	25	26	27	28	29	30	Mo.	Days	Days	Name
1																															1	30		Tishri
2											1	2	3	4	5	6	7	1	2	3	4	5	6	7	8	9	10	11	12	13	14	2	30	14	Heshvan
3	15	16	17	18	19	20	21	22	23	24	25	26	27	28	29	30	31	32	33	34	35	36	37	38	39	40	41	42	43	44	3	30	44	Kislev
4	45	46	47	48	49	50	51	52	53	54	55	56	57	58	59	60	61	62	63	64	65	66	67	68	69	70	71	72	73		4	29	73	Tevet
5	74	75	76	77	78	79	80	81	82	83	84	85	86	87	88	89	90	91	92	93	94	95	96	97	98	99	100	101	102	103	5	30	103	Shevat
6	104	105	106	107	108	109	110	111	112	113	114	115	116	117	118	119	120	121	122	123	124	125	126	127	128	129	130	131	132	133	6	30	133	Adar I
7	134	135	136	137	138	139	140	141	142	143	144	145	146	147	148	149	150	1	2	3	4	5	6	7	8	9	10	11	12		7	29	162	Aar II
8	13	14	15	16	17	18	19	20	21	22	23	24	25	26	27	28	29	30	31	32	33	34	35	36	37	38	39	40	41	42	8	30	192	Nisan
9	43	44	45	46	47	48	49	50	51	52	53	54	55	56	57	58	59	60	61	62	63	64	65	66	67	68	69	70	71		9	29	221	Iyyar
10	72	1	2	3	4	5	6	7	8	9	10	11	12	13	14	15	16	17	18	19	20	21	22	23	24	25	26	27	28	29	10	30	251	Sivan
11	30	31	32	33	34	35	36	37	38	39	40	1	2	3	4	5	6	7	1	1	2	3	4	5	6	7	1	1			11	29	280	Tammuz
12	2	3	4	5	6	7	1	2	3	4	5	6	7	8	9	10	11	12	13	14	15	16	17	18	19	20	21	22	23	24	12	30	310	Av
13	25	26	27	28	29	30	31	32	33	34	35	36	37	38	39	40	41	42	43	44	45	46	47	48	49	50	51	52	53		13	29	339	Elul
1		1	2	3	4	5	6	7	8	9	10	11	12	13	14	15	16	17	18	19	20	21	22	23	24	25	26	27	28	29	1	30	369	Tishri
2	30	31	32	33	34	35	36	37	38	39	40	41	42	43	44	45	46	47	48	49	50	51	52	53	54	55					2	29	398	Heshvan
																																	385	

when the key events of the flood took place. The "color coded" days in this calendar will be developed one at a time as we study the Genesis account of the flood. For now, notice again that using this calendar there is exactly 150 days between the 2nd month, 17th day and the 7th month, 17th day as is demanded by the scriptural record.

Notice again that: (1) The 385 day leap year calendar is being used to track the flood account (2) Adar I is the inter-calculated month of 30 days duration. It is always named the "Leap Year month". In the Genesis account of the flood, we have shown that it is numbered the 7th month, the month of Nisan is referred to as the 8th month, etc. This is an important observation as we will soon see. (3) Before Noah and his family entered the ark on Heshvan 10, the leap year had already gone through 39 days (Grey rows).

[1] *And the LORD said unto Noah, Come thou and all thy house into the ark; for thee have I seen righteous before me in this generation.*

[4] *For yet seven days, and I will cause it to rain upon the earth forty days and forty nights; and every living substance that I have made will I destroy from off the face of the earth* Genesis 7: 1,4

Noah was obviously a man of great faith. He was called *righteous* by God. The Lord commanded Noah and his family to enter into the ark on the 10th day of the 2nd month and remain there for 7 full days (10th day of 2nd month through the 16th day of 2nd month). During these 7 days, Noah and his sons were loading animals and supplies into the ark. Noah did not have to go out and round them up. God supernaturally gathered all of the animals, fowls and insects to Noah

[19] *And of every living thing of all flesh, two of every sort shalt thou bring into the ark, to keep them alive with thee; they shall be male and female.*
[20] *Of fowls after their kind, and of cattle after their kind, of every creeping thing of the earth after his kind,* **two of every sort shall come unto thee,** *to keep them alive*   Genesis 6:19-20

It is obvious that God abated the natural enmity between classes of animals, and changed them to trust Noah and his sons.

*And it came to pass **after** seven days, that the waters of the flood were upon the earth*   Genesis 7:10

Genesis 7:10 clearly states that *after* seven full days had elapsed the deluge of rain and subterranean waters began to flood the earth on the 8th day (Heshvan 17).

*In the six hundredth year of Noah's life, in the second month, the seventeenth day of the month, **the same day** were all the fountains of the great deep broken up, and the windows of heaven were opened*   Genesis 7:11

The great flood came upon the earth when Noah was 600 years old. This was in the 1057th year since Adam and Eve were cast out of the Garden of Eden. Hence, Noah was born 557 years after Adam left Eden, Adam lived to a ripe old age of 930 years old . Hence, Noah was a contemporary of Adam for about 457 years. The deluge began on Heshvan 17 which was the 2^{cd} month of a leap year.

*And the rain was upon the earth **forty days and forty nights***
Genesis 7:12

The fountains also of the deep and the windows of heaven were stopped, and the rain from heaven was restrained
Genesis 8:2

After 7 full days to load the ark, it began to rain and it rained for 40 full days and 40 full nights (17th day of 2nd month through the 26th day of 3rd month). The rain ended on Kislev 26.

[17] *And the **flood was forty days upon the earth;** and the waters increased, and bare up the ark, and it was lifted up above the earth.*

[24] *And the **waters prevailed upon the earth an hundred and fifty days*** Genesis 7:17, 24

Genesis 7:17 verifies that the flood was upon the earth for 40 full days. This does *not* mean that the earth was covered with water for only 40 days and nights, but that it rained for 40 days and nights. This is clear when we read the entire flood account. It rained for 40 days and 40 nights. The rain ceased on the 26th day of the 3rd month (Kislev) at 6:00 PM. the waters then continued to rise for 120 more full days: (40 +120)=150 days. The water *prevailed* upon the earth for 150 days. The Hebrew word for prevail is *gabar*, and it means to *exceed*, or to *dominate*. Taken literally, the rainwater was upon the face of the earth for a full 150 days before it started to evaporate.

*And the waters **prevailed**, and were increased greatly upon the earth; and **the ark went upon the face of the waters***
   Genesis 7:18

Genesis 7:17-18 records that the ark was lifted or floated just as it was designed to do as the rain fell. It *went upon the face of the waters.* The ark was probably built in the area of Babylon or Mesopotamia, and it was driven by the wind and waves until it reached the Mountains of Ararat (Genesis 8:5).

If the waters (Rain) stopped after 40 days and prevailed for 120 more days, how were the waters *increased greatly*? The answer is that all of the atmospheric water was poured out upon the earth, but so was all of the great subterranean oceans and vast aquifers. Evidently, the subterranean waters continued to surface and accumulate upon the earth through a full 150 days. At the end of 150 days, all waters ceased accumulating upon the earth and the waters began to recede.

[19] *And the waters **prevailed exceedingly** upon the earth; and **all the high hills**, that were under the whole heaven, were covered.*
[20] ***Fifteen cubits upward did the waters prevail;** and **the mountains were covered*** Genesis 7: 19-20

The waters floated the ark, and the ark *moved* upon the waters. The water rose until it covered the highest mountain peak by *15 cubits* (22.5 feet). The global and not local nature of the flood is confirmed here: *All the hills under heaven* were inundated (covered). Since the water peaked after 150 days had elapsed (Genesis 7:24), The highest level of water peaked as Nisan 17 ended.

And the waters returned from off the earth continually: and after the end of the hundred and fifty days the waters were abated   Genesis 8:3

This is a very difficult verse. Most authors say that this is just a confirmation of Genesis 7:24 and ignore it. However, Genesis 7:24 is referring to when the rains fell for 40 days, and the waters continued to rise for another 110 days from subterranean sources. Genesis 8:3 is referencing a different , subsequent time period in which the waters *returned from off the earth* for 150 days. The waters *abated* after 150 days. "Abated" is translated from the Hebrew word *chacer*, which is only used here in the flood narrative. It means to "decrease" or "fall". This is a second period of 150 days in which the waters decreased. The waters were abated after 314 days had elapsed from when the rains started to fall: The 314th day was on Av 20.

And the ark rested in the seventh month, on the seventeenth day of the month, upon the mountains of Ararat
       Genesis 8:4

This is a difficult passage and seems to be in direct conflict with Genesis 8:5 which states that:

And the waters decreased continually until the tenth month: in the tenth month, on the first day of the month, were the tops of the mountains seen   Genesis 8:5

The record clearly states that the *tops of mountains* were not seen until the *10th day of the 10th month*. So how could the ark *rest* upon Mt. Ararat on the 17th day of the 7th month? The following graphic will prove to be helpful in subsequent discussions.

Mo.	1	2	3	4	5	6	7	8	9	10	11	12	13	14	15	16	17	18	19	20	21	22	23	24	25	26	27	28	29	30	Mo.	Days	Days	Name
1																															1	30		Tishri
2											1	2	3	4	5	6	7	1	2	3	4	5	6	7	8	9	10	11	12	13	2	30	14	Heshvan
3	15	16	17	18	19	20	21	22	23	24	25	26	27	28	29	30	31	32	33	34	35	36	37	38	39	40	41	42	43	44	3	30	44	Kislev
4	45	46	47	48	49	50	51	52	53	54	55	56	57	58	59	60	61	62	63	64	65	66	67	68	69	70	71	72	73		4	29	73	Tevet
5	74	75	76	77	78	79	80	81	82	83	84	85	86	87	88	89	90	91	92	93	94	95	96	97	98	99	100	101	102	103	5	30	103	Shevat
6	104	105	106	107	108	109	110	111	112	113	114	115	116	117	118	119	120	121	122	123	124	125	126	127	128	129	130	131	132	133	6	30	133	Adar I
7	134	135	136	137	138	139	140	141	142	143	144	145	146	147	148	149	150	1	2	3	4	5	6	7	8	9	10	11	12		7	29	162	Aar II
8	13	14	15	16	17	18	19	20	21	22	23	24	25	26	27	28	29	30	31	32	33	34	35	36	37	38	39	40	41	42	8	30	192	Nisan
9	43	44	45	46	47	48	49	50	51	52	53	54	55	56	57	58	59	60	61	62	63	64	65	66	67	68	69	70	71		9	29	221	Iyyar
10	72	1	2	3	4	5	6	7	8	9	10	11	12	13	14	15	16	17	18	19	20	21	22	23	24	25	26	27	28	29	10	30	251	Sivan
11	30	31	32	33	34	35	36	37	38	39	40	1	2	3	4	5	6	7	1	2	3	4	5	6	7	1		1			11	29	280	Tammuz
12	2	3	4	5	6	7	1	2	3	4	5	6	7	8	9	10	11	12	13	14	15	16	17	18	19	20	21	22	23	24	12	30	310	Av
13	25	26	27	28	29	30	31	32	33	34	35	36	37	38	39	40	41	42	43	44	45	46	47	48	49	50	51	52	53		13	29	339	Elul
1		1	2	3	4	5	6	7	8	9	10	11	12	13	14	15	16	17	18	19	20	21	22	23	24	25	26	27	28	29	1	30	369	Tishri
2	30	31	32	33	34	35	36	37	38	39	40	41	42	43	44	45	46	47	48	49	50	51	52	53	54	55					2	29	398	Heshvan

385

Genesis 8:4 actually records that the Ark rested *not* upon Mt. Ararat as is frequently claimed, but above the *Mountains of Ararat*. The "Mountains of Ararat" in Genesis refer to a general region, not any specific mountain. The Jewish historian Josephus wrote:

> The ark grounded on the top of a certain mountain in Armenia .The Armenians call this place, αποβατηριον or *The Place of Descent*; for the ark being saved in that place, its remains are shown there by the inhabitants to this day. Now all the writers of barbarian histories make mention of this flood, and of this ark; among whom is **Berossus**. For when he is describing the circumstances of the flood, he goes on thus: "It is said there is still some part of this ship in Armenia, at the mountain of the Cordyaeans; and that some people carry off pieces of the bitumen, which they take away, and use chiefly as amulets for the averting of mischiefs." Hieronymus the Egyptian also, who wrote the Phoenician Antiquities, and Mnaseas, and a great many more, make mention of the same. Nay, Nicolaus of Damascus, in his ninety-sixth book, hath a particular relation about them; where he speaks thus: "There is a great mountain in Armenia, over Minyas,

called Baris, upon which it is reported that many who fled at the time of the Deluge were saved; and that one who was carried in an ark came on shore upon the top of it; and that the remains of the timber were a great while preserved". (*Antiquities of the Jews*,I.3.5-6)

The event of Genesis 8:5 (1st day of the 10th month, occurred *after* the 150 days that the waters *increased*, but 78 days *before* the second period of 150 days ended. The waters abated (ceased to accumulate) on the 20th day of the 12th month.

However, Genesis 8:5 states that the waters *returned from off the earth* (not disappeared, but evaporated and receded) until *after the end* of *another* 150 days. The Hebrew word for *returned* is שוב and it means to *bring back or restore*. The word translated *abated* is the Hebrew word *chacer*. This word only occurs *once* in the Holy bible and it is in Genesis 8:3. It means to *lesson or lower*. The proper interpretation is that Genesis 8:3 means that *after* the 150 days that the waters rose, the waters began to recede. After 78 days, the Ark *rested* at that time over the Mountains of Mt. Ararat. The Hebrew word for rested is *shabath*. It means *to repose or be still*. Genesis 8:3 should be interpreted to mean that the ark became *stationary* over the Mountains of Ararat on the 17th day of the 7th month. This harmonizes with Genesis 8:5 that says the tops of the mountains were seen 72 days later. If the ark had been grounded 78 days earlier on Shevat 1 Noah would have felt the ark cease to rock upon the waves, look out, and see the top of the mountain it grounded upon. The biblical scholar Don Roth (http://www.biblicalcalendarproof.com) agrees with this interpretation and stated that after the ark was tossed and moved about by the rain and rising waters for 150 days that it

64

became *stationary* over the Mountains of Ararat 78 days later. It remained there until it finally grounded as the waters receded. Certainly, God would need to move the ark from Mesopotamia to somewhere over the Mountains of Ararat before it grounded, so this is a believable interpretation. The Mountains of Ararat (Armenia) are in northern Turkey, and they are more than 600 miles from where the ark was built. Over the 40 days of downpour, and driven by great waves that were caused by geological chaos from the waters of the deep, the ark was tossed and turned upon the waves for another 110 days until the water reached its maximum depth.

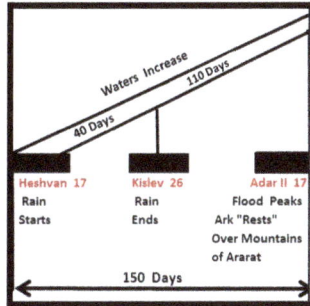

Waters Increase

110 Days

40 Days

Heshvan 17
Rain
Starts

Kislev 26
Rain
Ends

Adar II 17
Flood Peaks
Ark "Rests"
Over Mountains
of Ararat

150 Days

The scriptures say it *moved upon the waters*. The wind and waves obviously pushed the ark more than 600 miles to the west of where it was built. The text says that the ark then *rested upon* the *Mountains of Ararat*. The Hebrew word translated *upon* in Genesis 8:4 is a derivative of the word *on* or *'al* in Hebrew. This word means one of two things: *against, touching* or as *over/above*. The Hebrew word for *rested* in Genesis 4:8 means to recline/stay. Don Roth has done an extensive investigation of Genesis 8:4 and has reached the following conclusion.

"What is meant by the word *rested* in Genesis 8:4? The Hebrew word "rested" in Genesis 8:4 is defined in Strong's Concordance (#5117) as "the stopping of movement or activity". It is the same word used in Exodus 20:11 when "God rested on the 7th day". The use of this word in

Genesis 8:4 simply tells us the ark had ceased rolling and plunging through turbulent waters caused by the great deluge. The wind and waves which had driven the ark for more than 600 miles ceased and the water became calm. The ark had not come to the Mountains of Ararat by mere chance, but it rested over the mountains in preparation for grounding; God had supernaturally placed it there"
http://www.biblicalcalendarproof.com/Hebrew Calendar/DonRoth

The Hebrew description and position of Genesis 4 suggests that that the ark became stationary over the Mountain range of Mt. Ararat in modern day Turkey. The waters had increased for 150 days until the highest mountain was covered with 15 cubits of water (22.5 feet). The highest peak in the Ararat range is about 17,000 feet but Mt. Everest is over 29,000 feet high. If the flood covered all of the land, the ark could not possibly have run aground after 150 days had elapsed. The ark ceased its movement across the waters on the 17th day of the 7th month, and that is what we choose to believe. It did not actually rest upon ground until the 1st day of the 10th month (Genesis 8:5). Note from the following graphic that the 7th month is the extra

Mo.	1	2	3	4	5	6	7	8	9	10	11	12	13	14	15	16	17	18	19	20	21	22	23	24	25	26	27	28	29	30	Mo.	Days	Name	Days
1																															1	30	Tishri	
2				1	2	3	4	5	6	7	1	2	3	4	5	6	7	8	9	10	11	12	13	14							2	30	Heshvan	14
3	15	16	17	18	19	20	21	22	23	24	25	26	27	28	29	30	31	32	33	34	35	36	37	38	39	40	41	42	43	44	3	30	Kislev	44
4	45	46	47	48	49	50	51	52	53	54	55	56	57	58	59	60	61	62	63	64	65	66	67	68	69	70	71	72	73		4	29	Tevet	73
5	74	75	76	77	78	79	80	81	82	83	84	85	86	87	88	89	90	91	92	93	94	95	96	97	98	99	100	101	102	103	5	30	Shevat	103
6	104	105	106	107	108	109	110	111	112	113	114	115	116	117	118	119	120	121	122	123	124	125	126	127	128	129	130	131	132	133	6	30	Adar I	133
7	134	135	136	137	138	139	140	141	142	143	144	145	146	147	148	149	150														7	29	Aar II	150

Heshvan 10... Noah entered the Ark (10th Day of 2nd Month)

Heshvan 16...God sealed the Ark (16th Day of 2nd Month)

Heshvan 17...Rain starts to fall (17th Day of 2nd Month)

Kislev 26...Rain ceases on 26th Day of 3rd Month

Adar II 17..... Flood reaches its maximum level On 17th Day of the 7th Month

month Adar II which only occurs in a leap year.

Authors Note: The months of the Hebrew/Jewish calendar were not named until after the Babylonian exile of 70 years, more than 3000 years later. The months prior to that time were simply numbered.

As demanded by scripture, the 150th day from when it started to rain on the 2nd month, 17th day falls on the 17th day of the 7th month.

This result can *only* be true using a 385 day Hebrew leap year, or a calendar with 3 out of the first 4 months containing 30 days and one month containing 29 days. The length of the 5th month can be of 29,30 or 31 days. Only one calendar is known to ever existed with these characteristics and that is the Hebrew Lunar/ solar calendar with the year of the flood being a Leap Year with 385 days. *This is strong proof that the calendar in use at the time of the flood, and before the flood, could have been the same calendar in use today*. In fact, it is a testimony to the omnipotence of God that this would be true. In any case, it is obvious that both before and after the great flood a calendar to predict both the cycles of the moon and the seasons was needed to support a pre-flood agricultural society. It should also be noted that such a calendar was *critical* to predict and observe the 7 Feasts of Israel which God commanded to be kept at a specific time each year over 1000 years later. This is a testimony to the omnipotent nature of Jehovah.

*And the waters **decreased continually** until the tenth month: in the tenth month, on the first day of the month, were the tops of the mountains seen*   Genesis 8:5

The waters increased for 150 days, and then they began to recede on the 18th day of the 7th month (Adar I 18). On the 1st day of the 10th (Sivan 1) month Noah looked out and could see the mountain tops around him for the first time since water covered the earth. Logic would demand that this is true. The waters rose for 150 days, and then peaked after covering the highest mountain to a depth of 15 cubits. With no rain or upheaval of water from the depths of the earth, the water then

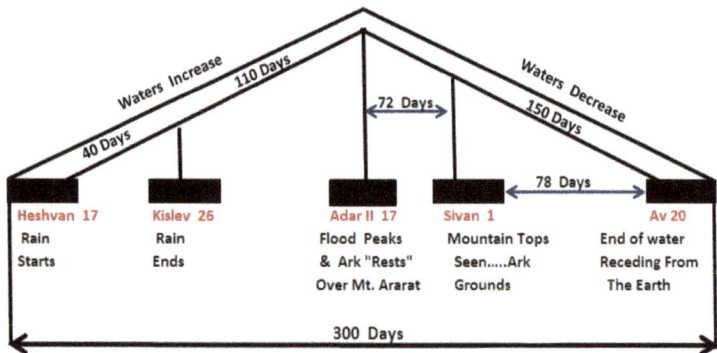

Heshvan 17	Kislev 26	Adar II 17	Sivan 1	Av 20
Rain	Rain	Flood Peaks	Mountain Tops	End of water
Starts	Ends	& Ark "Rests"	Seen.....Ark	Receding From
		Over Mt. Ararat	Grounds	The Earth

started to recede for another 150 days. The following graphic shows the first 300 days of the flood.

On the 1st day of the 10th month, the tops of mountains were seen by Noah. This was 73 days after the ark had rested or became stationary on the 17th day of the 7th month.

Note: there have been several expeditions to Mt. Ararat which have proposed to find the remains of the ark on the side of the mountain encased in ice. The Holy Bible strongly suggests that if the ark is ever going to be found, it will not be on the top of the mountain called Mt. Ararat. The Biblical record only states that the ark became stationary over the mountains (mountain range) called Ararat. No wonder the ark has never been found, it is likely that archeologists are looking in the wrong place! The exact location of where the ark grounded is only known by God.

[5] *And the waters decreased continually until the tenth month: in the tenth month, on the first day of the month, were the tops of the mountains seen*   Genesis 8:5

When the ark finally grounded (the mountain tops were then seen), Noah waited another 40 days (2^{cd} day of 10th month through the 11th day of the 11th month). The graphic illustrates the first 262 days of the flood, beginning with the first day that the rain began to fall on the 17th day of the 2^{cd} month.

Mo.	1 2 3 4 5 6 7 8 9 10 11 12 13 14 15 16 17 18 19 20 21 22 23 24 25 26 27 28 29 30	Mo.	Days	Name	Days
1		1	30	Tishri	
2	1 2 3 4 5 6 **7** 1 2 3 4 5 6 7 8 9 10 11 12 13 14	2	30	Heshvan	14
3	15 16 17 18 19 20 21 22 23 24 25 26 27 28 29 30 31 32 33 34 35 36 37 38 39 **40** 41 42 43 44	3	30	Kislev	44
4	45 46 47 48 49 50 51 52 53 54 55 56 57 58 59 60 61 62 63 64 65 66 67 68 69 70 71 72 73	4	29	Tevet	73
5	74 75 76 77 78 79 80 81 82 83 84 85 86 87 88 89 90 91 92 93 94 95 96 97 98 99 100 101 102 103	5	30	Shevat	103
6	104 105 106 107 108 109 110 111 112 113 114 115 116 117 118 119 120 121 122 123 124 125 126 127 128 129 130 131 132 133	6	30	Adar I	133
7	134 135 136 137 138 139 140 141 142 143 144 145 146 147 148 149 **150** 1 2 3 4 5 6 7 8 9 10 11 12	7	29	Aar II	162
8	13 14 15 16 17 18 19 20 21 22 23 24 25 26 27 28 29 30 31 32 33 34 35 36 37 38 39 40 41 42	8	30	Nisan	192
9	43 44 45 46 47 48 49 50 51 52 53 54 55 56 57 58 59 60 61 62 63 64 65 66 67 68 69 70 71	9	29	Iyyar	221
10	72 1 2 3 4 5 6 7 8 9 10 11 12 13 14 15 16 17 18 19 20 21 22 23 24 25 26 27 28 29	10	30	Sivan	251
11	30 31 32 33 34 35 36 37 38 39 40			11	29	Tammuz	262

1 — Heshvan 10... Noah entered the Ark (10th Day of 2nd Month)
7 — Heshvan 16...God sealed the Ark (16th Day of 2nd Month)
1 — Heshvan 17...Rain starts to fall (17th Day of 2nd Month)
40 — Kislev 26...Rain ceases on 26th Day of 3rd Month
150 — Adar II 17..... Flood reaches its maximum level On 17th Day of the 7th Month
72 — Sivan 1......Tops of Mountains are seen on 1st Day of 10th Month
40 — Tammuz 11.....Noah has waited 40 days for the waters to recede (Sivan 2-Tammuz 11)

God had caused rain to fall for 40 days and 40 nights and He also opened up the subterranean aquifers to increase water upon the earth until the highest mountain was covered by 15 cubits of water. For 150 days the waters upon the earth increased. As the waters reached its peak on the 17th day of the 7th month, they began to slowly decrease for another 150 days.

The sun dried the waters and the subterranean cavities began to refill. After 72 days, Noah could see the tops of mountains from the ark's position over the Mountains of Ararat on the 1st day of the 10th month (Sivan 1). Noah waited 40 more days for the waters to recede, and on the 12th day of the 11th month

Mo.	1	2	3	4	5	6	7	8	9	10	11	12	13	14	15	16	17	18	19	20	21	22	23	24	25	26	27	28	29	30	Mo.	Days	Name	Day
1																															1	30	Tishri	
2						1	2	3	4	5	6	7	1	2	3	4	5	6	7	8	9	10	11	12	13	14					2	30	Heshvan	14
3	15	16	17	18	19	20	21	22	23	24	25	26	27	28	29	30	31	32	33	34	35	36	37	38	39	40	41	42	43	44	3	30	Kislev	44
4	45	46	47	48	49	50	51	52	53	54	55	56	57	58	59	60	61	62	63	64	65	66	67	68	69	70	71	72	73		4	29	Tevet	73
5	74	75	76	77	78	79	80	81	82	83	84	85	86	87	88	89	90	91	92	93	94	95	96	97	98	99	100	101	102	103	5	30	Shevat	103
6	104	105	106	107	108	109	110	111	112	113	114	115	116	117	118	119	120	121	122	123	124	125	126	127	128	129	130	131	132	133	6	30	Adar I	133
7	134	135	136	137	138	139	140	141	142	143	144	145	146	147	148	149	150	1	2	3	4	5	6	7	8	9	10	11	12		7	29	Aar II	162
8	13	14	15	16	17	18	19	20	21	22	23	24	25	26	27	28	29	30	31	32	33	34	35	36	37	38	39	40	41	42	8	30	Nisan	192
9	43	44	45	46	47	48	49	50	51	52	53	54	55	56	57	58	59	60	61	62	63	64	65	66	67	68	69	70	71		9	29	Iyyar	221
10	72	1	2	3	4	5	6	7	8	9	10	11	12	13	14	15	16	17	18	19	20	21	22	23	24	25	26	27	28	29	10	30	Sivan	251
11	30	31	32	33	34	35	36	37	38	39	40	41	42	43	44	45	46	47	48	49	50	51	52	53	54	55	56	57	58		11	30	Tammuz	280
12	59	60	61	62	63	64																									12	30	Av	286

1 Heshvan 10... Noah entered the Ark (10th Day of 2nd Month)

7 Heshvan 16...God sealed the Ark (16th Day of 2nd Month)

Heshvan 17...Rain starts to fall (17th Day of 2nd Month)

40 Kislev 26...Rain ceases on 26th Day of 3rd Month

150 Adar II 17..... Flood reaches its maximum level On 17th Day of the 7th Month

72 Sivan 1.......Tops of Mountains are seen on 1st Day of 10th Month

40 Tammuz 11....Noah has waited 40 days for the waters to recede (Sivan 2-Tammuz 11)

41 Tamuz 12....Noah sends out a raven and a dove (12th Day of 11th Month)

49 Tamuz 21.....Noah sends out a dove for 2nd time (21st Day of 11th Month)

57 Tamuz 29.....Noah sends out a dove for 3rd time (29th Day of 11th Month)

(Tammuz 12) Noah opened the window of the ark.

[6] *And it came to pass at the end of forty days, that Noah opened the window of the ark which he had made:*

[7] *And he sent forth a raven, which went forth to and fro, until the waters were dried up from off the earth.*

[8] *Also he sent forth a dove from him, to see if the waters were abated from off the face of the ground;*

[9] *But the dove found no rest for the sole of her foot, and she returned unto him into the ark, for the waters were on the face of the whole earth: then he put him into the ark.*

[10] *And he stayed yet other seven days; and again he sent*

forth the dove out of the ark;
[11] *And the dove came in to him in the evening; and, lo,*
in her mouth was an olive leaf pluckt off: so Noah
knew that the waters were abated from off the earth.
[12] *And he stayed yet other seven days; and sent forth the*
dove; which returned not again unto him anymore
Genesis 8: 6-12

Here we must be very careful in reconstructing the sequence of events which took place.

Noah waited until the end of 40 days. This demands that the next sequence of events begin on the 12th day of the 11th month (Tammuz 12). on this day Noah opened a window of the ark and sent out a raven and a dove. The raven was stronger than the dove and had more range to fly. The raven went forth until the waters were dried up from the earth and did not return to the ark, but the dove did return. How long was the dove gone? This is not directly revealed, but we will assume that it was less than 24 hours (1 day). This is believed to be true based upon the record of Genesis 8:10-11. After Noah released the dove and the raven he waited yet another 7 days. Most biblical scholars have assumed that the dove was gone for 7 days because of the adjective yet, but the phrase yet another does not imply precedence but simply states he waited another 7 days. In any case, after the dove returned Noah definitely waited another 7 days, and he released a 2cd dove. He sent forth the dove and it returned to him in the evening. Now, why was this phrase added to the narrative? I believe that it was to indicate that the dove had been released as daylight appeared in early morning (a reasonable assumption) and returned to the ark that same evening. There is no way to prove this assumption, but anyone

71

who has hunted doves knows that a dove will fly in short intense bursts, and that they do not possess the stamina that a raven possesses. Continuous flight for 12 or more hours would be reasonable for a little dove. This is certainly not a critical or limiting assumption.

The dove returned to Noah in the evening with an olive leaf, so Noah assumed that the waters had abated and dried up somewhere. Note that this is not definite proof of this conclusion, the dove could have found a floating olive branch. So Noah waited another 7 days and released a dove for the 3rd time. This time the dove did not return so Noah knew that the dove had landed and stayed somewhere.

An interesting question is: Why did Noah choose to send a raven and a dove? The answer might lie in the symbolism and prophetic nature of the ark. The Old Testament contains many symbolic references to a coming Messiah and redeemer who we now know was Jesus Christ. The raven is a dark and sinister bird who lives on the flesh and meat off dead animals. Genesis 8:7 tells us that the raven went to and fro. Most expositors have interpreted this as the raven flying back and forth to the ark until it finally did not return. This notion is, I believe incorrect. The raven flew to and fro upon the waters until the waters dried up. The raven could have alighted and fed upon a dead animal, since there was likely a lot of floating carcasses. It is more believable that the raven and dove were released at the same time, but only the dove returned. The dove is a clean animal which would not light on dead bodies, so being tired of searching for land it returned to rest at the ark.

The nature of the raven and dove can be contrasted to people in the world today. Sinful man who have no belief in Jesus Christ seek the carrion and rotting flesh of the world. They have no problem seeking out the sinful world that surrounds us. They fly from one unclean and sinful practice to another, never really finding the peace and love of Jesus Christ. The dove is a universal symbol of the Holy Spirit. The Holy Spirit fell like a dove upon Jesus Christ when He was baptized by John the Baptist in the River Jordan. The was released by Noah a total of 3 times, and 3 is the number of completeness. After the dove was released the third time and failed to return, Noah knew that the dove had rested somewhere. Jesus said, come unto Me and I will give you rest (Matthew 11:28). The dove returned to Noah 2 times, and this is a type of how God has dealt with mankind. There are two bodies of Holy scripture which compose the Bible: The Old Testament and the New Testament. Both speak of Jesus Christ as the coming Messiah in the Old Testament and the redeemer of sins who came in the New Testament.

The dove was sent three times by God, who was a shadow and type of God sending the Holy Spirit to His believing remnant. The First Dove: In the Old Testament the Holy Spirit (dove) came upon men and women of faith as God willed, to accomplish specific goals and purposes. The Second Dove: The second dove represented the 3.5 year ministry of Jesus Christ here on earth. The dove returned a second time carrying an Olive Branch. The olive branch represented new life. The dove returning with news of new life reminds us of the good news of Jesus Christ. Christ the Son of God came to give us eternal life. He died upon the Cross of Calvary, rose from the dead after 3 days and 3 nights, and He then left us the Holy Spirit as a guarantee of His promises. The 3rd time that the dove was released, it did not return. There is coming a day when men will seek Jesus Christ but they will not find Him. Christ said: I am the door: by me if any man enter in, he shall be saved, and shall go in and out, and find pasture (John 10:9). However, Christ is the one who will shut the open door, just as God shut the door to the Ark, and all who would not believe perished. Jesus Christ is our Ark of safety.

[15] *And they went in unto Noah into* **the ark,** *two and two of all flesh,* **wherein is the breath of life.**
[16] *And they that went in, went in male and female of all flesh, as God had commanded him: and* **the LORD shut him in**   Genesis 7:15-16.

When the ark was filled, God shut the door and the rest of the world who was outside of the mercy and grace of God received the Wrath of God. It will be that way once again when Christ suddenly appears to execute judgment upon an unbelieving world. Christ spoke of this time when He taught the Parable of the wise and foolish virgins in Matthew 25.

.....the bridegroom came; and they that were ready went in with him to the marriage: and **the door was shut.**   Matthew 25:10

Those who were not in the bosom of Jesus Christ were shut out, and Jesus spoke the terrifying final words: Verily I say unto you, I know you not (Matthew 7:22-23).

[13] *And it came to pass in the six hundredth and first year, in the first month, the first day of the month, the waters were dried up from off the earth: and Noah removed the covering of the ark, and looked, and, behold, the face*

74

of the ground was dry.
[14] And in the second month, on the seven and twentieth
day of the month, was the earth dried
Genesis 8:13-14

Mo.	1	2	3	4	5	6	7	8	9	10	11	12	13	14	15	16	17	18	19	20	21	22	23	24	25	26	27	28	29	30	Mo.	Days	Name	Days
1																															1	30	Tishri	
2							1	2	3	4	5	6	7	1	2	3	4	5	6	7	8	9	10	11	12	13	14				2	30	Heshvan	14
3	15	16	17	18	19	20	21	22	23	24	25	26	27	28	29	30	31	32	33	34	35	36	37	38	39	40	41	42	43	44	3	30	Kislev	44
4	45	46	47	48	49	50	51	52	53	54	55	56	57	58	59	60	61	62	63	64	65	66	67	68	69	70	71	72	73		4	29	Tevet	73
5	74	75	76	77	78	79	80	81	82	83	84	85	86	87	88	89	90	91	92	93	94	95	96	97	98	99	100	101	102	103	5	30	Shevat	103
6	104	105	106	107	108	109	110	111	112	113	114	115	116	117	118	119	120	121	122	123	124	125	126	127	128	129	130	131	132	133	6	30	Adar I	133
7	134	135	136	137	138	139	140	141	142	143	144	145	146	147	148	149	150	1	2	3	4	5	6	7	8	9	10	11	12		7	29	Aar II	162
8	13	14	15	16	17	18	19	20	21	22	23	24	25	26	27	28	29	30	31	32	33	34	35	36	37	38	39	40	41	42	8	30	Nisan	192
9	43	44	45	46	47	48	49	50	51	52	53	54	55	56	57	58	59	60	61	62	63	64	65	66	67	68	69	70	71		9	29	Iyyar	221
10	72	1	2	3	4	5	6	7	8	9	10	11	12	13	14	15	16	17	18	19	20	21	22	23	24	25	26	27	28	29	10	30	Sivan	251
11	30	31	32	33	34	35	36	37	38	39	40	41	42	43	44	45	46	47	48	49	50	51	52	53	54	55	56	57	58		11	29	Tammuz	280
12	59	60	61	62	63	64	65	66	67	68	69	70	71	72	73	74	75	76	77	78	1	2	3	4	5	6	7	8	9	10	12	30	Av	310
13	11	12	13	14	15	16	17	18	19	20	21	22	23	24	25	26	27	28	29	30	31	32	33	34	35	36	37	38	39		13	29	Elul	339
1	40	1	2	3	4	5	6	7	8	9	10	11	12	13	14	15	16	17	18	19	20	21	22	23	24	25	26	27	28	29	1	30	Tishri	369
2	30	31	32	33	34	35	36	37	38	39	40	41	42	43	44	45	46	47	48	49	50	51	52	53	54	55	56				2	29	Heshvan	395
																																		385

1 — Heshvan 10... Noah entered the Ark (10th Day of 2nd Month)...600th Year of Noah's Life

7 — Heshvan 16...God sealed the Ark (16th Day of 2nd Month)

17 — Heshvan 17...Rain starts to fall (17th Day of 2nd Month)

40 — Kislev 26...Rain ceases on 26th Day of 3rd Month

150 — Adar II 17..... Flood reaches its maximum level On 17th Day of the 7th Month

72 — Sivan 1.......Tops of Mountains are seen on 1st Day of 10th Month

40 — Tammuz 11.....Noah has waited 40 days for the waters to recede (Sivan 2-Tammuz 11)

41 — Tamuz 12.....Noah sends out a raven and a dove (12th Day of 11th Month)

49 — Tamuz 21.....Noah sends out a dove for 2nd time (21st Day of 11th Month)

57 — Tamuz 29.....Noah sends out a dove for 3rd time (29th Day of 11th Month)

78 — Av 21.......78 Days after Noah saw the mountain tops,

40 — Tishri 1....Earth is "dry , Chareb" (1st Day of 1st Month)...601st Year of Noah's Life

Heshvan 27...Earth is "dry, Yabesh" (27th Day of 2nd Month)...601st Year of Noah's Life

Heshvan 28...... Noah Departs the Ark (27th Day of 2cd Month)... 601st year of Noah's Life

The biblical record records in Genesis 8:13 that on the 1st day of the 1st month in the 601st year of Noah that Noah looked out and the earth was dry. Then, in the very next verse we are told in Genesis 8:14 that on the 27th day on the 2cd month in the 601st year of Noah that the earth had dried. These seemingly conflicting statements are actually not in conflict at all. In Genesis 8:13 the Hebrew word for dry is chareb; which means "an absence of water, dry". The Hebrew word translated as dried in Genesis 8:14 is yabesh; which means "shriveled or withered due to a lack of moisture". In Genesis 8:13 the condition of the earth was that there was no standing water and the earth is dry but the ground was saturated and soggy. In Genesis 8:14 the condition of the earth is hard, dried and absent of water. This is an example of why anyone wanting to interpret the inerrant, holy words of God in the Bible must link the Latin, Greek or English version of the Holy scriptures back to the Aramaic/ Hebrew (Old Testament) or the original Greek (New Testament) manuscripts. The interpretation or meaning in the original manuscripts is what gives rise to different versions of the modern English bibles such as The American Standard Version (1901), The NIV (1978) and the Amplified Bible (1965).

The tops of mountains were seen by Noah on the 1st day of the 10th month (Sivan 1). On the 28th day of the 11th month (Tammuz 28) the dove that Noah sent out from the ark failed to return. Water fell or decreased over a 150 day period of time between the 18th day of the 7th month (Adar II 18) and the 20th day of the 12th month: Exactly 40 days later, the earth was dry but saturated on the 1st day of the 1st month. On the 27th day of the 2nd month (Heshvan 27), 56 days later, the earth had become cracked and dried.

On the 28th day of the 2nd month in the 601st year of Noah, he left the ark and stood on dry land for the first time in 395 days. Note that from Genesis 8:15 that Noah did not make the decision to leave the ark on his own: God commanded him to do so. This reminds us of the 3.5 year ministry of Jesus Christ.

Jesus Christ repeatedly said that He did nothing on His own, but only did those things that the Father told Him to do (John 5:19, 30). So it was with Noah: We see Noah's obedient life demonstrated in his willingness to obey without question the Lord's commands regarding the ark (Genesis 6:22; 7:5, 9; 8:18).

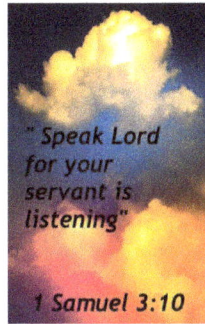

" *Speak Lord for your servant is listening*"

1 Samuel 3:10

Consider that Noah and his generation more than likely had never seen rain before, yet God tells Noah to build a large seagoing vessel nowhere near a body of water. Noah's trust in God was such that he promptly obeyed. Noah's blameless life is made manifest as he obeys the Lord in light of the approaching day of wrath. The apostle Peter tells us that Noah was a "herald of righteousness" (2 Peter 2:5), and the author of Hebrews says that he "condemned the world" (Hebrews 11:7) through his righteous actions. Noah always faithfully obeyed the Lord (www.Got questions.org).

The story of Noah would not be complete without remembering what Noah did as soon as he left the ark.

[20] *And Noah builded an altar unto the LORD; and took of every clean beast, and of every clean fowl, and offered burnt offerings on the altar.*

[21] *And the LORD smelled a sweet savour; and the LORD said in his heart, I will not again curse the ground any more for man's sake; for the imagination of man's heart is evil from his youth; neither will I again smite any more everything living, as I have done*
                    Genesis 8: 20-21

Noah was a man of great faith, just as Abraham, Joseph, David and other Old Testament saints were great men of faith. They are remembered in the great faith chapter; Hebrews 11. However, all were sinners and needed a redeemer that would someday appear to forgive their sins forever. All had one thing in common, they sought grace and mercy from God and offered up sacrifices of praise and worship. The first thing that Noah did when he left the ark was to build an altar and offer burnt offerings to the Lord. The burnt offerings rose to God a sweet savor, and it pleased the Lord. In an act of grace, He promised Noah that He would never again curse the ground as He had done when Adam and Eve sinned, and that He would never again smite everything living upon the earth. A nonbeliever would say, Aha... God has lied because in Revelation 21 God destroys the earth. However, careful study of this last act of God will reveal that He has removed all believers and all unbelievers from the face of the earth prior to destruction by fire.

Chapter 4

The Post- Flood World

Noah had waited 173 days after the ark had rested over the Mountains of Ararat for the earth to dry enough to support his animal cargo. Noah also probably needed the earth to begin its season of agricultural recovery to sustain his animals and fowls. However, the decision of when the time was right to leave the ark was not up to Noah. God had protected them and kept them for 395 days and Noah had faith in God to finish what He had started. Finally God came to Noah on the morning of the 396th day, Heshvan 28.

[15] *And God spoke unto Noah, saying,*
[16] *Go forth of the ark, thou, and thy wife, and thy sons, and thy sons' wives with thee.*
[17] *Bring forth with thee every living thing that is with thee, of all flesh, both of fowl, and of cattle, and of every creeping thing that creepeth upon the earth; that they may breed abundantly in the earth, and be fruitful, and multiply upon the earth.*
[18] *And Noah went forth, and his sons, and his wife, and his sons' wives with him:*
[19] *Every beast, every creeping thing, and every fowl, and whatsoever creepeth upon the earth, after their kinds, went forth out of the ark*   Genesis 8:15-19

Only 121 years earlier, God had grieved that He had created man, and He had declared that He would destroy everything upon the earth but a remnant that He would choose.

79

[5] *And GOD saw that the wickedness of man was great in the earth, and that every imagination of the thoughts of his heart was only evil continually.*
[6] *And it repented the LORD that he had made man on the earth, and it grieved him at his heart.*
[7] *And the LORD said, I will destroy man whom I have created from the face of the earth; both man, and beast, and the creeping thing, and the fowls of the air; for it repenteth me that I have made them*   Genesis 6:5-7

The Hebrew word for *repented* is *nacham*, and it means to "breath Heavily", to be "sorry". We learn much about God in these few verses.

(1) Man was not created by a random act of nature: God made man.

(2) Creationalists boldly proclaim that all animals, birds, fish and critters miraculously appeared and evolved. God made man, and beast, and the creeping thing, and fowls of the air

(3) When God looked down upon man, He saw nothing but *wickedness* and *evil*. Many Christians staunchly maintain that God is love and will forgive. This is only a partial understanding of who God is and His eternal nature. God cannot tolerate sin, and although He is *longsuffering that none should perish* (II Peter 3:9) God said that *My spirit shall not always strive with man* (Genesis 6:3). God is surely a God of Love: *For God so loved the world that He sent His only begotten son, that whosoever believes upon Him shall not perish but have eternal life* (John 3:16). But do not be deceived, God will turn away from man if provoked long enough.

(4) God is a spirit being, but He has a *heart* and He has feelings; He *grieved.* Oh how His heart must have ached as He watched His only Son cry out to Him as a man: *My God, My God...Why hast thou forsaken me?* Oh the unsearchable riches of a father who would give His only Son for me ...and for you.

God had played God, and He sent a flood upon the face of the earth. But *where sin abounds, much more does grace abound* (Romans 5:20). The flood was over but Noah and his family had been spared. The earth must now be repopulated and the remnant that survived must have been relatively free from sin. However, Noah and his family still had the curse of Adam and Eve upon them. The sin nature might have been temporarily minimized, but it was still there. The way that man and animals were to live upon the earth and even the way the earth looked would change forever when the waters receded.

Noah Leaves the Ark

Noah had been sealed in the ark for 395 days and it was time to leave . It must have been both a sad and glad occasion. Noah was no doubt glad to finally be free of his small room on the ark, and he was ready to begin a new life on a new earth. But Noah was no doubt sad, because as he looked out over the land and every living thing upon the face of the earth had drowned, and the land which had been covered for over a year with water was parched and brown. He was also sad because everything that he had worked for over many years was gone; his house, all of his worldly possessions, his barn and flocks... all gone. The first obvious task would be to build a new house for him and his family, but what did he do? He built an altar for the Lord and

81

prepared to offer up sacrifices of praise and worship to Jehovah God.

*And Noah builded an **altar** unto the LORD; and took of every clean beast, and of every clean fowl, and offered **burnt offerings** on the altar*   Genesis 8:20

It is easy to miss the incredible story contained in this one verse. Scientists have estimated that about 6000 different species of animals had entered the ark. We know that there were 7 pairs of each clean animal and 2 pairs of each unclean animal. It is not known how many species of clean animals had been put on the ark, but it must have been a large number. Instead of taking a hike or basking in the sun after being cooped up for so long, Noah built an *altar* of sacrifice to the Lord and then offered up a sacrifice of *every clean animal and fowl*. The one thing that set Noah, Abraham, David and all of the old testament patriarchs apart from everyone else was their *faith* and *love* of the Lord. It was not that they were perfect, for God points out in the scriptures many times how they committed sin. The thing that set them apart was their contrite nature after committing a sin, and their understanding of *grace*. Oh, help us to learn something today from those great men of God that lived and died thousands of years ago.

And the LORD smelled a sweet savour   Genesis 8:21-a

God *smelled a sweet savour*: This reminds us of the Tabernacle in the wilderness that was built by Moses and the Children of Israel. In the Tabernacle was a holy place which was just outside of the Holy of Holies, separated by a thick gold and purple veil. In front of the veil stood the Altar of Incense. The priesthood would every day take coals from the Altar of Sacrifice which

82

stood at the tabernacle gate, and place these coals upon the *Altar of Incense*. He would then offer up a sweet savour sacrifice unto the Lord, and if everything was done right the Lord would be pleased.

On one day of the year, The *Feast of Atonement*, the High Priest would wash himself and appear ritually clean before the Altar of Incense. He would then offer up burning incense which would pass over the veil and fill the Holy of Holies with a sweet savour. This was necessary before the High Priest could enter into the Holy of Holies and make atonement for the sins of the people. He would sprinkle the blood of a sacrificial lamb upon the Horns of the *Ark of the Covenant* and plead for mercy and grace. It is certain that this is exactly what Noah did as he sacrificed clean animals and fowl to the Lord. It is not revealed how Noah knew which animals were clean and which were unclean, since the law and the rituals of the tabernacle were not yet given. But, we can be sure that God gave him that knowledge.

; and the LORD said in his heart, I will not again curse the ground any more for man's sake; for the imagination of man's heart is evil from his youth; neither will I again smite any more everything living, as I have done
                    Genesis 8:21-b

This is a covenant that God made with Noah when He smelled the sweet savour of has burnt offering. The Hebrew word for covenant means a pledge or a promise. When Adam sinned and was forced out of the garden of Eden, God cursed the land and caused thistles and thorns to grow there (Genesis 3:17-19). God then reassured Noah that He would not again *smite every living thing* as He had done by the flood.

83

It is more than interesting that God next assured Noah that the seasons of the year would continue forever to govern the planting, harvest and reaping cycles of agriculture.

While the earth remaineth, seedtime and harvest, and cold and heat, and summer and winter, and day and night shall not cease
Genesis 8:22

Dietary Restrictions

Prior to the flood, the descendents of Adam and Eve were evidently vegetarians: at least it appears that God had given mankind no authority to eat the flesh of animals or birds, or even to eat of any creature that lived in rivers, lakes or the sea (Genesis 3:18-19). No scripture in the Bible reveals that God gave any commands to Adam or his progeny allowing the consumption of meat. This is not proof that it was forbidden to eat meat, but the clear dietary instructions given to Adam and Eve indicate that this was the case.

In the sweat of thy face shalt thou eat bread, till thou return unto the ground; for out of it wast thou taken: for dust thou art, and unto dust shalt thou return   Genesis 3:19

Those who have studied the Book of Genesis might ask why Genesis 4:2 states that Abel was a keeper of sheep. Abel may have been raising sheep for sacrifices to the Lord, or he might have used the wool to make winter clothes. We do know that 3 times before the flood we read that God told man to eat of the fruit and vegetables that grew out of the land, but never once did He say that eating meat was acceptable. We also know that there is no record that mankind existed in enmity with the animal kingdom before the great flood.

84

Before the flood, the descendents of Noah depended upon the seasons to plant and harvest crops. This is a clue that a lunar/solar calendar must have been in place by divine instructions from God to signal when to seed and harvest. The first time that the seasons are mentioned in the Holy Scriptures is in the creation account.

And God said, Let there be lights in the firmament of the heaven to divide the day from the night; and let them be for signs, and for seasons, and for days, and years Genesis 1:14

Recall that the first thing that Noah did when he left the ark was to build an altar to the Lord and then offer up burnt offerings to the Lord. The burnt sacrifice was a sweet savour to the Lord (Genesis 8:20). God was obviously pleased and He made the following covenant promise to Noah.

While the earth remains, seedtime and harvest, and cold and heat, and summer and winter, and day and night shall not cease Genesis 8:22

Notice that the condition on God's promise is while the earth remains. God is not promising that the earth will remain forever. He is saying that the seasons (Summer and Winter) will not be interrupted as they were during the flood while the earth remains in existence. We know that one day, this world will again be destroyed by fire (II Peter 3:10).

When Adam and Eve were created and placed into the Garden of Eden, God commanded them to replenish the earth.

*And God blessed them, and God said unto them, Be fruitful, and multiply, and **replenish** the earth, and subdue it: and have*

85

dominion over the fish of the sea, and over the fowl of the air,
and over every living thing that moveth upon the earth
Genesis 1:28

It is fascinating and possibly never noticed that God
commanded Adam and Eve to replenish the earth. Is this a
tantalizing clue that the earth was once filled with ape-like
creatures that were like humans but did not possess a spiritual
soul, hmmm. In any case, God now gives to Noah and his sons
that exact same command except He did not tell them to have
dominion over the animals, fowl and fish.

And God blessed Noah and his sons, and said unto them, Be
fruitful, and multiply, and replenish the earth Genesis 9:1

God next appears to change the basic relationship between
man and the animal kingdom.

[2] *And the fear of you and the dread of you shall be upon every*
beast of the earth, and upon every fowl of the air, upon
all that moves upon the earth, and upon all the fishes
of the sea; into your hand are they delivered.
[3] *Every moving thing that lives shall be meat for you; even as*
the green herb have I given you all things.
[4] *But flesh with the life thereof, which is the blood*
thereof, shall ye not eat Genesis 9:2-4

God directly addresses Adam at this point in time and tells him
that from that point on, the beasts of the field will fear man; but
every creature on the land, in the sea and in the air are given to
man to eat. The only prohibition is that blood cannot be
consumed. This restriction is later repeated when the law is
given to Moses and the Children of Israel.

For it is the life of all flesh; the blood of it is for the life thereof: therefore I said unto the children of Israel, Ye shall eat the blood of no manner of flesh: for the life of all flesh is the blood thereof: whosoever eateth it shall be cut off   Leviticus 17:14

In the Garden of Eden, it is written in the ancient Book of Jubilees that Adam and Eve actually spoke with the animals, and there was no fear between men and animals. It is believed that this relationship between man and the animals continued to a lesser degree through the Adamic Dispensation that ended at the flood. It is likely that man could only communicate with animals in a very limited sense such as commanding Fido to sit. It is not logical that God would specifically address this relationship between man and the lower levels of creation after the flood if it had previously existed before the flood. In any case, animals would be at enmity with man from that point on: The wild animal kingdom would fear man and instinctively flee from sinful man. Recall that man was now allowed to hunt and kill wild animals for food, but it would not be easy.

A Judicial Command

We next see a judicial command that God gave to Noah.

Whoso sheddeth man's blood, by man shall his blood be shed: for in the image of God made he man...   Genesis 9:6

In case you missed it, God instituted capital punishment for anyone who willfully and maliciously takes the life of another person. Since God does not change His mind because of His omnipotence, this is a clear authorization of capital punishment today for 1st degree murder. Those who oppose capital punishment and claim that it is against God's will simply have

87

not read and understood Genesis 9:6. Murder is to be punished by death. Under the Law of Moses (God's Law) which came much later, there is a commandment: Thou shalt not kill. Obviously, this is speaking of killing another man or woman, not an animal. Breaking this commandment was punishable by death when it was broken. In fact, if anyone living under the law broke even one of the 613 commandments they had broken all of the law. Willfully breaking any of the ten commandments carried a death penalty (Hebrews 10:28).

If one will study the full council of the scriptures, it is clear that under certain circumstances there is not necessarily a death penalty. This is a mystery, but when Cain slew Abel he was not killed by God but banished to live in the wilderness forever. King David was guilty of adultery and murder, both punishable by death, but because of his repentance God forgave him of his sins (II Samuel 11 and 12). The woman taken in the act of adultery was still under the law, but when she was brought to Jesus the lack of two or more accusers allowed Jesus to send her way forgiven (John 8:3-11). Unknown to most people, these scriptural truths are the basis of modern trial by jury, and the commutation of a death penalty in favor of life in prison.The world before the flood had been populated with the direct descendants of Adam and Eve. In the short space of 1657 years, mankind had morphed from a completely sinless world to a world in which GOD saw that the wickedness of man was great in the earth.

every imagination of the thoughts of (their) heart was only evil continually   Genesis 6:5

The Lifespan of Post-Flood Humans

The world before the flood had been populated with the direct descendants of Adam and Eve. In the short space of 1657 years, mankind had morphed from a completely sinless world to a world in which GOD saw that the wickedness of man was great in the earth, and that *every imagination of the thoughts of (their) heart was only evil continually* (Genesis 6:5). Before the flood, the years that man lived were substantially more than after the flood. This is generally contributed to one of two cause and effects: (1) The bodies of Adam and Eve while they lived in the Garden of Eden were perfect and there was no degradation due to the Tree of Life and the absence of germs and sickness.

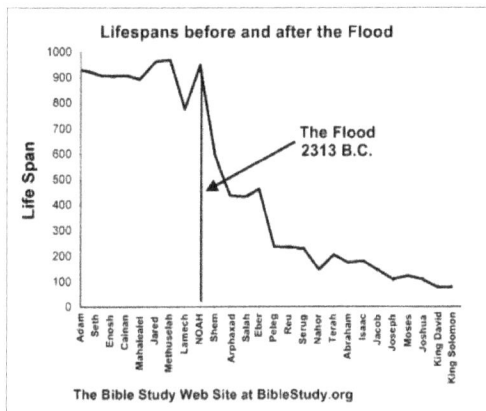

Lifespans before and after the Flood

The Flood 2313 B.C.

The Bible Study Web Site at BibleStudy.org

The world before the flood had been populated with the direct descendants of Adam and Eve. In the short space of 1657 years, mankind had morphed from a completely sinless world to a world in which GOD saw that the wickedness of man was great in the earth, and that *every imagination of the thoughts of (their) heart was only evil continually* (Genesis 6:5). Before the flood, the years that man lived were substantially more than after the flood. This is generally contributed to one of two cause and effects: (1) The bodies of Adam and Eve while they lived in

89

the Garden of Eden were perfect and there was no degradation
due to the Tree of Life and the absence of germs and sickness.
The progeny of Adam and Eve would inherit the genetic
structure of Adam and Eve. Gradually, this would be overcome.
(2) The earth was protected by a canopy of mist which blocked
the degrading effects of ultraviolet rays and direct sunlight. The
first assumption would no doubt be true, but the second is
questionable. Was Adam and Eve protected by a canopy of
mist? What do the scriptures say?

Rain or No Rain ?

[5] *And every plant of the field before it was in the earth, and
every herb of the field **before it grew**: for the LORD God
had not caused it to rain upon the earth, and there was
not a man to till the ground.*
[6] *But there went up **a mist** from the earth, and watered the
whole face of the ground*
Genesis 2:5-6

The creative work of God prior to the formation of Adam and
Eve was finished in 7 days. (Genesis 1:1-31). Genesis 2: 1-15
describes how God prepared both the earth and the Garden of
Eden for habitation. Genesis 2:5-6 records that every tree, bush
and herb was created within the earth but had not yet sprung
up.

The reason is clearly given: There was *no man to till the ground*
and *no rain had fallen* upon the earth. The Lord did not cause it
to rain, but commanded that a *mist* rise up from the earth, and
this mist as it rose formed water (dew) and nourished the flora,
fauna and crops. It was not until this cycle was in place that God
(1) Created Adam and Eve and (2) Created the Garden of Eden

for them to live. It is tempting to say that there was no rain while Adam and Eve were in the Garden of Eden, but all that can really be said is that no rain had fallen up to that time. Many will argue that this mist continued to be the only source of atmospheric water until the time of the Flood. The Holy record does not require it to be the only source of water after Adam's creation. Presence of mist prior to Adam's creation does not preclude the existence of or the need for rain after he was created nor after his fall from the Garden of Eden until the flood came.

There is another clue and it concerns the *sign* which God gave Noah that the world and its inhabitants would never be flooded again. This sign was a *rainbow* in the sky.

[13] *I do set my bow in the*
    cloud, and it shall be
    for a token of a
    covenant between me
    and the earth.

[14] *And it shall come to pass, when I bring a cloud over the*
    earth, that the bow shall be seen in the cloud
                Genesis 9:13

Rainbows can be observed whenever there are drops of water in the air and sunlight passes through these drops at a low angle of observation. The rainbow is also commonly seen near waterfalls or fountains. The atmospheric conditions that cause a rainbow to appear does not require it to rain. It is certain that rivers and waterfalls existed before the flood, and a rainbow could have occasionally appeared. The rainbow was set into the clouds by God, and the same God that created earth and man could certainly have delayed the visibility of a rainbow until after the flood. It might have also been true that the rainbow had always existed, but after the flood God gave it as a perpetual sign from that point on that He would never again destroy the world with water.

In summary, It is not wise to state biblical truth based upon the absence of knowledge even if it seems logical. However, the weight of evidence is enough to conjecture that it did not rain prior to Noah's flood, but that weather conditions afterte Great Flood were exactly as they are today.

Noah Lived in An Agricultural Society

It is interesting that when Adam and Eve were expelled from the Garden of Eden they not only left a perfect living environment, but from that moment on they had to work for their food. The descendents of Adam became farmers and an agricultural society. Cain was the first farmer identified by name.

[3] *And in process of time it came to pass, that Cain brought of the fruit of the ground an offering unto the LORD.*
[4] *And Abel, he also brought of the firstlings of his flock and of the fat thereof. And the LORD had respect unto Abel and to his offering*   Genesis 4:3-4

Cain and many others became farmers and tilled the land. The mist which watered the Garden of Eden may or may not have been a part of the post-Edenic world. Agricultural crops had to be watered both before and after the flood. The Bible does *not* specifically tell us whether or not it had rained before the Flood.

Noah seemed to understand what rain was when God mentioned it to him (Genesis 7:4-5).

The Condition of Mankind

The state of mankind before the flood was decidedly wicked. Sin in itself would have been enough to cause God to destroy everything that lived upon land to perish, but there was another thing that happened that prompted Him to execute this unprecedented catastrophe.

[8] *But Noah found grace in the eyes of the LORD.*
[9] *These are the generations of Noah: Noah was a just man and perfect in his generations, and Noah walked with God*   Genesis 6:8-9

It is interesting that God called Noah perfect in his generations. Since Noah had committed sin (Romans 3:23); why would God make this statement? In the original Hebrew text, the word translated as perfect is *tamiym* (Strong's #8549), and its basic meaning is "complete" or "entire." It does not mean "perfect" as we think of it today, that is "without fault, flaw, or defect." There are other English words that are better translated from tamiym such as "whole," "full," "finished," "well-rounded," "balanced," "sound," "healthful," "sincere," "innocent," or "wholehearted." When God stated that Noah was tamiym He did not mean that Noah had never sinned, but that he was spiritually mature and that he had a wholehearted, healthy relationship with God. While Noah was found tamiym in Gods sight, the offspring which followed were not. Just as Cain had chosen to sin and rebel against God, descendents of Noah followed the same path of death and destruction. The first

93

record of rebellion is found in a most unusual place...... In the
house of Noah.

The Sin of Noah and His Sons

[18] *And the sons of Noah, that went forth of the ark, were*
Shem, and Ham, and Japheth: and Ham is the father of
Canaan.

[19] *These are the three sons of Noah: and of them was the*
whole earth overspread.

[20] *And Noah began to be an husbandman, and he planted a*
vineyard:

[21] *And he drank of the wine, and was drunken; and he was*
uncovered within his tent.

[22] *And Ham, the father of Canaan, saw the nakedness of his*
father, and told his two brethren without.

[23] *And Shem and Japheth took a garment, and laid it upon*
both their shoulders, and went   backward, and covered
the nakedness of their father; and their faces were
backward, and they saw not their father's nakedness.

[24] *And Noah awoke from his wine, and knew what his*
younger son had done unto him.

[25] *And he said, Cursed be Canaan; a servant of servants shall*
he be unto his brethren.

[26] *And he said, Blessed be the LORD God of Shem; and*
Canaan shall be his servant.

[27] *God shall enlarge Japheth, and he shall dwell in the tents of*
Shem; and Canaan shall be his servant.

[28] *And Noah lived after the flood three hundred and fifty*
years   Genesis 9:18-28

This story of Noah and his descendants has two important aspects. *First*, is it clearly reveals that although Noah found grace in God and was called *righteous*, he was a man who like everyone else was born with the sin nature imputed from Adam and Eve; and he was not immune from unrighteous acts. Upon leaving the ark, Noah started an agricultural society. He and his sons were allowed to kill animals and eat meat (no blood), but there were likely few animals to eat for several years. At some point in time, probably many years later since he had grandsons. *Second*, Noah planted a vineyard and made wine. Having revived the ancient practice of making wine, he proceeded to get drunk. In his drunken state, he obviously made his way to his bed and passed out naked. The youngest son of Noah, who was Ham, apparently entered into his father's tent when Noah was drunk, asleep, and naked. Some commentators have suggested Ham committed some sexual misdeed with Noah but this is not likely. His sin was more likely that he boasted to his brothers about seeing their father naked and laughed at his grandfather, thus dishonoring Noah. Shocked and alarmed, Japheth and Shem took a robe, walked backwards into the tent, and covered their father, but they did not allow themselves to see him naked. Upon waking, Noah realized the full impact of what had taken place, and he called a family meeting. In the confrontation something strange occurs: Noah says nothing to Ham, but he picks out one of Ham's sons, Canaan, to rebuke (Genesis 10:6). The incident is difficult to understand: Why did Noah not rebuke Ham instead of Canaan? After all, it was clearly Ham who laughed and ridiculed his father. The best explanation seems to be that Noah saw a moral weakness in Ham, and that it would somehow be propagated by Canaan. Perhaps Canaan upon hearing the news from his father

Ham also laughed at Noah and made fun of his grandfather....
we may never know. In any case, the wrath of Noah was
directed to Canaan and not Ham. As a direct result of this curse,
the line of Canaan turned out to be terribly wicked and sinful.

The curse on Canaan and his descendants also dictated that
they were destined to be *servants of servants*. In other words,
they would occupy the lowest rank in society, serving those who
themselves are servants. This is not necessarily implying slavery.
Many have used this curse to justify slavery of black people.
However, they fail to notice that the curse was directed to
Canaan, whose descendants occupied what is now Israel.

The descendants of Canaan were *Canaanites*. According to
Genesis 10:15-20, they were the people who dwelt in Phoenicia
and in the Land of Canaan. They became a tribe of sinful and
morally corrupt people. This is apparent from passages such as
Genesis 15:16; 19:5; Leviticus 18 and 20 and Deuteronomy
12:31. By the time of Abraham the measure of their iniquity
was already full. By the time of the entrance of Israel into
Canaan under Joshua, the Canaanites, who were also called the
Amorites, were ripe for divine judgment by God. Sodom and
Gomorrah were largely populated by the Canaanites who
practiced incest and homosexuality throughout the city.

Having addressed Canaan, Noah next turned his attention to
Shem, Ham and Japheth. Noah blessed Shem (Genesis 9:26–27),
and it was through Shem that the redeemer promised to Adam
would come (Genesis 3:15). The ancestral tree of Christ is traced
back through Abraham, Judah, and David (Luke 3:36) to Shem.

Japheth was the oldest son of Noah, and he sired Gomer,
Magog, Madai, Javan, Tubal, Meshech and Tiras (Genesis 10:2).

The descendants of Shem became the people who migrated to the north and west, settling what is today Russia, Germany, Poland and surrounding countries. Descendants of Ham's other children occupied the land of Africa.

The key question is: *Why was Noah so angry that Ham saw him naked?* Surely in the close confines of the ark there was little privacy and Ham was a son of Noah. It seems that there is more here than meets the eye. Some have proposed that Ham and/or Canaan actually did something to Noah in addition to seeing him naked. The passage mentions that Noah *knew what his youngest son had done to him* (Genesis 9:24) when he sobered up. Whatever happened to Ham's father and Canaan's grandfather lay before them naked is not revealed in scripture. The severity of Noah's curse certainly implies that Canaan was somehow involved in a sordid incident. Ham clearly saw his father naked and drunk, but covered his nakedness with his back turned. Any theory as to what actually occurred is speculation.

It is not stated in the scriptural records, but it is reasonable speculation that the entire incident caused a "family split" and that the three clans struck out on their own to the regions previously mentioned. From the widespread dispersion of each tribe, the area called Mesopotamia was settled, but how were other continents settled and how did other languages, dialects and cultures arise in the western hemisphere.

The Progeny of Noah

Noah was given a command by God to *Be fruitful, and multiply, and replenish the earth* (Genesis 9:1). It is commonly taught (correctly) that every person on the earth came from Adam and

97

Eve, but it is also true that the entire human race was birthed by Noah, his wife, his three sons and their wives. Noah had three sons named Japheth, Ham and Shem. All three were on board the ark during the great flood. It was from these three sons and their wives that the population of the earth as we know it today evolved. Of particular interest to us are how the different races on the earth today were spawned, and how did they get so geographically dispersed after the flood?

The biblical records make it quite clear that the diversity between ethnic groups of people that exist today came from Japheth, Shem and Ham.

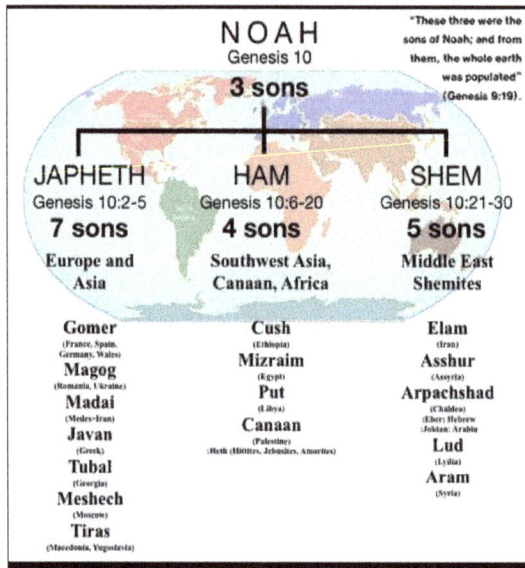

God must have caused genetic development of different groups of people in different areas to evolve into different colors and physical characteristics.

Before we discuss this evolution as revealed in the Book of Genesis, we can address the different dialects and languages which evolved with some confidence and authority. After the flood, God instructed Noah and his three sons to *Be fruitful and multiply, and fill the earth* (Genesis 9:1,7). Japheth had 7 sons, Ham had 4 and Shem had 5. Shortly after Noah and his three sons left the ark, an event occurred which would shape the destiny of these three sons and their progeny.

The Dispersion of Mankind

Some have postulated that following the deluge there were temporary land bridges between Europe and Ataractic/Canada. From there, migrations would have taken people (and animals) to the Western hemisphere and on to Antarctica. However, the scriptures reveal that God himself was directly involved in forming the diversity of people in the world today. In Genesis 11 we are told that:

[1] *And the whole earth was of one language, and of one speech.*
[2] *And it came to pass, as they journeyed from the east, that they found a plain in the land of Shinar; and they dwelt there.*
[3] *And they said one to another, Go to, let us make brick, and burn them throughly. And they had brick for stone, and slime had they for morter.*
[4] *And they said, Go to, let us build us a city and a tower, whose top may reach unto heaven; and let us make us a name, lest we be scattered abroad upon the face of the whole earth.*
[5] *And the LORD came down to see the city and the tower,*

which the children of men builded.

[6] *And the LORD said, Behold, the people is one, and they have all one language; and this they begin to do: and now nothing will be restrained from them, which they have imagined to do.*

[7] *Go to, let us go down, and there **confound their language**, that they may not understand one another's speech.*

[8] *So **the LORD scattered them abroad** from thence **upon the face of all the earth**: and they left off to build the city.*

[9] *Therefore is the name of it called Babel; because the LORD did there **confound the language of all the earth**: and from thence did **the LORD scatter them abroad upon the face of all the earth***   Genesis 11:1-9

Ancient historical records confirm that Noah had a great grandson called Nimrod, who was the son of Cush. The Bible records that he was a mighty hunter before the Lord and that he.... began to be mighty in the earth. He had a reputation as a king who was rebellious against God, and he wanted to rise up a tall monument above the earth in an effort to be like God. He built a tremendous structure called the Tower of Babel which rose above the plains of a place called Shinar.   Genesis 11 reveals that Nimrod and those who lived in Shinar all spoke the same language, which might be expected since they all were descendents of Noah. When God saw what had been done, it angered him. Rather than destroy them in His

righteous anger, He instead (1) Confused (*confounded*) their language and (2) *Scattered them abroad upon the face of the earth*. There you have it! For the biblical literalist, this solves the mystery of how people settled and developed all over the world after the great flood. This does not at all destroy the concept of evolution. In different places with different environments (Antarctica, Amazon Jungle, Yucatan Peninsula, etc.) it is natural that man would adopt and morph to different external features. There is no conflict between evolution and divine actions that scattered the people. The lord caused them to speak different languages and to live in different places.

The Covenant God Made With Noah

There is some confusion over the covenant that God made with Noah and the commands that God gave Noah. The following commands that God gave to Noah have been previously discussed, but are listed here for continuity.

- God commanded Noah and his sons to *Be fruitful, and multiply, and replenish the earth* (Genesis 9:1,7)

- Beast of the field are delivered to Noah and his descendants for food (no blood may be consumed), but there will be fear between man and beast (Genesis 9:2-3)

- If a man willingly and intentionally commits murder he shall put to death (Genesis 9:5-6)

A covenant is a *promise* or an agreement that is generally made between two parties. A covenant between God and man is an agreement with much stronger conditions. There are two kinds of covenants that can be made between two parties: (1) Unconditional and (2) Conditional. A *conditional* covenant is one in which both parties agree to the conditions and if one or the other party breaks the condition(s), the covenant is null and void. An unconditional covenant also involves conditions, but not necessarily negotiated between the two parties. The one who sets the condition(s) is bound to honor the covenant no matter what the other party might do or say. When God makes an unconditional covenant with some man He will honor the promise made no matter what the other party might do or say. The covenant with Adam was *conditional*. God promised Adam that he could remain in the Garden of Eden forever, but only if he never ate of the fruit of the Tree of knowledge between good and evil. When Eve ate of the fruit and Adam did likewise, he was cast out of the Garden of Eden. God made a promise to Noah which was *unconditional*.

And I will establish my **covenant** *with you; neither shall all flesh be cut off any more by the waters of a flood; neither shall there anymore be a flood to destroy the earth*   Genesis 9:11

The Covenant with Noah was that when the lightning crashed and the rain fell that he need not be afraid; water and floods would never again destroy the earth. God promised Noah that this would never happen again. Notice that God did not say that He would never destroy the world and everything in it again. Peter reveals to us that the world will be destroyed/renovated once again, but this time by fire.

[6] *Whereby the world that then was, being overflowed with water, perished:*

[7] *But the heavens and the earth, which are now, by the same word are kept in store, reserved unto fire against the day of judgment and perdition of ungodly men.*

[10] *But the day of the Lord will come as a thief in the night; in the which the heavens shall pass away with a great noise, and the elements shall melt with fervent heat, the earth also and the works that are therein shall be burned up* II Peter 3: 6-7,10

The covenant with Noah was ratified with a *sign*....a rainbow.

[13] *I do set my bow in the cloud, and it shall be for a token of a covenant between me and the earth.*
[14] *And it shall come to pass, when I bring a cloud over the earth, that the bow shall be seen in the cloud:*
[15] *And I will remember my covenant, which is between me and you and every living creature of all flesh; and the waters shall no more become a flood to destroy all flesh* Genesis 9: 13-15

[5] *And every plant of the field before it was in the earth, and every herb of the field before it grew: for the LORD God had not caused it to rain upon the earth, and there was not a man to till the ground.*
[6] *But there went up a mist from the earth, and watered the whole face of the ground* Genesis 2:5-6

Genesis 2:5-6 was written immediately following the 6 days of work during which God created the heavens and the earth. On the 3rd day God created herbs and fruit trees, and by the end of the 7th day all flora and fauna needed water. To water the earth, a mist rose up. A rainbow usually occurs when the rays of the sun are refracted through droplets of rain in a cloud, but a rainbow is frequently seen in the mist that rises from a waterfall. Genesis 2:5 only makes a specific statement: There had been no rain upon the earth during the creative process. When the mist appeared, it is likely that a rainbow could have been seen, but it was just a "pretty phenomenon".

God might have simply designated the rainbow as a *sign of His covenant* with Noah and to all the generations that followed. Of course, God can make anything happen and He also might have initiated the natural phenomenon known as a rainbow after the flood. Either way, the sign of a rainbow remains today.

Chapter 5

Prophetic Gleanings

The biblical story of the ark is perhaps the best known story in the bible to children of all ages. The ark is often pictured (inaccurately) as a playground for animals while a great rain fell over all of the earth. As we have carefully studied Noah and the ark, a more accurate and detailed story of what actually happened and why it happened is revealed. The story of Noah's ark is far more important than it might first appear. It will be shown in this chapter that the ark was a detailed and prophetic picture of Jesus Christ the Son of God. Jesus Christ was the promised messiah who would one day arise to redeem all of the Old Testament saints who believed in faith that God would one day send a redeemer who would take away their sins. The faith of Noah, Abraham, Jacob and Joseph was a cornerstone of all who be saved through the ages by the same type of faith. All New Testament believers are said to be true children of Abraham.

[6] *Even as Abraham believed God, and it was accounted to him for righteousness.*
[7] *Know ye therefore that they which are of faith, the same are the children of Abraham.*
[8] *And the scripture, foreseeing that God would justify the*

heathen through faith, preached before the gospel
unto Abraham, saying, In thee shall all nations be
blessed.
[9] *So then they which be of faith are blessed with faithful*
Abraham Galatians 3:6-9

Many Christians assume that the Old Testament was just a historical record of a different dispensation and not worthy of detailed study. Every Christian should understand that the *entire Bible* is about Jesus Christ. If we carefully study we can find Him on every page of the Holy Bible, not just in the New Testament but also in the Old Testament. *Here I am our Lord said,: it is written about me in the scroll* (Hebrews 10:7). God used a great flood to destroy a sinful world, but by grace He rescued Noah and his family from death and destruction. Noah was saved in the same way that every Christian today is saved; by faith. The ark is in every way representative of Jesus Christ the long awaited Messiah of the Old Testament patriarchs and the Jewish people. It is often stated that Jesus Christ was not revealed to people in the Old Testament, but this is simply not true. The Old Testament contains over 500 references to Jesus Christ as the coming Messiah, not by name but by signs and prophecy. The Old Testament prophets wrote under the influence of the Holy Spirit where he would be born; His virgin birth; His sacrificial death on the cross and many more things.

One other place we can find Jesus in the Old Testament is in what we call *types*. A "type" is an example or illustration that points to another person or an event. *Typology* in Christian theology and Biblical exegesis is an example or event in the Old Testament which points to a corresponding event or fulfillment in the New Testament. Most types in the Old Testament are those which point to a fulfillment of some promise or appearance of Jesus Christ in the New Testament. The bible is full of *types* and *antitypes*. The realization of a type is called the antitype. One of the main purposes of the Old Testament is to reveal the future coming of Jesus Christ as the redeemer of sins . Finding Jesus hidden in type is a most exciting and rewarding study. As it is recorded in Proverbs 25:2, *It is the glory of God to conceal a matter, but the glory of kings is to search out a matter.* So let us study Noah's Ark as a type of Jesus Christ and see what we can discover.

1.0 Jesus Christ is our Ark of Salvation

The ark was a place of refuge by which Noah, his family and a cargo of creatures were saved from the Wrath of God. It was offered to all mankind, but only a remnant believed and by faith were saved from death and destruction. Jesus Christ is our *ark of salvation*, and by believing upon His Holy name all who accept Him as their Lord and Savior will be saved. The ark was offered to Noah and his family by God and He gave Noah all that was necessary to save him and his family. Christ was sent by God to redeem all of mankind, and His redeeming work on the cross is sufficient to save all who would believe upon His holy name. Those who believe in faith will be saved from death and destruction through Him just as the ark protected and sustained Noah and His family. Jesus Christ will protect and redeem us today if we will believe upon His promises.

107

2.0 God Himself Sealed (Protected) the Ark With Pitch

God told Noah to *pitch it within and without with pitch* (Genesis 6:14). *Pitch* was a substance used to waterproof the ark. The Hebrew word used for pitch is *Kopher* which means *atonement*. The basic concept of Kopher carries two meanings. One is a *covering*, the other is *reconciliation*. In the Old Testament the Levitical Sacrificial system was set into place not to forgive sins, but to cover sins until sin could be permanently forgiven through the sacrificial death of Jesus Christ on the cross of Calvary. When Christ shed His precious blood upon the cross He took away all the sins of man. He did not abolish sin, but He was both the perfect, sinless sacrifice and the sacrificer for sin. *He who knew no sin became sin for us* (II Corinthians 5:21).

[17] *Therefore if any man be in Christ, he is a new creature: old things are passed away; behold, all things are become new.*

[18] *And all things are of God, who hath reconciled us to himself by Jesus Christ, and hath given to us the ministry of reconciliation;*

[19] *To wit, that God was in Christ, reconciling the world unto himself, not imputing their trespasses unto them; and hath committed unto us the word of reconciliation.*

[20] *Now then we are ambassadors for Christ, as though God did beseech you by us: we pray you in Christ's stead, be ye reconciled to God.*

[21] *For he hath made him to be sin for us, who knew no sin;*

108

that we might be made the righteousness of God in him.
II Corinthians 5:17-21

*And almost all things are by the law purged with blood; and
without shedding of blood is no remission*   Hebrews 9:22

Jesus permanently forgave our sins on the cross. The pitch
covered the ark and protected the people and animals inside
from the Wrath of God.

3.0 God Gave Ample Warning That Judgment Was Coming

God told Noah that a flood (the Wrath of God)
was coming upon a sinful and wicked earth. He
gave plenty of notice that the flood was coming
120 years before it came. *And the LORD said,
My spirit shall not always strive with man, for
that he also is flesh: yet his days shall be an
hundred and twenty years* (Genesis 6:3). Many
expositors have stated that this was a curse upon mankind, and
that man would live no longer than 120 years old. This is not
correct, since after the flood there were many who lived well
past 120 years old (Genesis 11). The context of this declaration
by God was that man had become wicked and sinful, and that
God was grieved that He had made man in his own image. The
ark was in plain view of everyone during the many years it was
under construction. It was a visible sign that a day of death and
destruction was coming soon. God in His grace and mercy gave
man a warning to repent and be saved from both physical and
spiritual death. This is a perfect *type* of what is going on today.
God is *longsuffering that none should perish*, but we have been
warned in the Book of Revelation that His Wrath upon the earth
is coming once again. Before the Wrath of God falls upon sinful

man, Christ will resurrect the dead and rapture out the saints who have believed and look forward to his second coming. At this time, God will again destroy all who will not accept Jesus Christ as their savior, and rescue those who will accept salvation and eternal life by believing upon His Son and the sacrifice He made for our sins upon the cross of Calvary. *Warning*: The time must be drawing near.

4.0 The Ark Was Constructed With Only One Door

The Ark which Noah built had only one door... One way into the safety and protection that God had provided. Christ used a door to confirm that He was the only way, the truth and the life.

I am the door: by me if any man enter in, he shall be saved, and shall go in and out, and find pasture   John 10:9

Christ had earlier pictured himself as the good Sheppard who is the door for his sheep (believers). In ancient Israel, there were two kinds of pens for sheep. The first would be found in the interior of every city and town, large enough to hold many sheep (A type of Jews and Gentiles). It was cared for by a porter or gate keeper. The porter would stand by the door and call the sheep into safety. In those cases when flocks of sheep came regularly to the enclosure, they would hear and recognize the gatekeeper; they were called by name and the good Sheppard knew them. As he called, they would respond and enter. The second kind of pen was found out in the field and was made of boulders and rock. The only entrance would sometimes not have a gate, and so the good Sheppard would lay in the entrance at night to protect his sheep. The Sheppard was literally the *door*. When wolves and predators sought entrance to the pen as a thief at night, the Sheppard would risk his life to protect his sheep. Jesus said:

I am the good shepherd: the good shepherd giveth his life for the sheep   John 10:11

Jesus used this earthly image to convey three important truths. The *first* is that God has a sanctuary, a safe place to bring His sheep. Once gathered there, He will save and keep them safe forever. *Second*, the only way to get into this place is through its one and only door: Jesus Christ. The only access we have to God is through Christ, and Him alone. *Third*, like the good Sheppard He would willingly laid down His life for us

5.0 God Told Noah to Make a Window For The Ark

A *window shalt thou make to the ark, and in a cubit shalt thou finish it above* (Genesis 6:16). It is possible that the ark had only one window. In Genesis 6:16 God told Noah to *make a window* for the ark, implying that there was to be only one window. Then, in Genesis 8:6 we read that Noah *opened the window* of the ark, once again implying only one window. It was to be finished *from above.*

He that cometh from above is above all: he that is of the earth is earthly, and speaketh of the earth: he that cometh from heaven is above all   John 3:31

Noah and his family were not to look down or around for their salvation, they were to look up towards heaven. In the same way the believer is to keep his eyes focus on Jesus and not on the world around him.

6.0 The Ark Had Three Levels

The ark was constructed with three decks …..*with lower, second, and third stories shalt thou make it* (Genesis 6:16). The universe which God made is composed of 3 different realms: The 1st, 2nd and 3rd heavens. The 1st heaven is the atmosphere that surrounds the planet earth: The 2nd heaven is the stars, planets and galaxies that are called outer space. The 3rd heaven is where God dwells. The apostle Paul was caught up into the 3rd heaven while he was still alive on earth, and there he saw things so incredible that he was not allowed to speak of them. It is not well understood, but after the *Old Earth* is purified and renovated, it will become the *New Earth*.

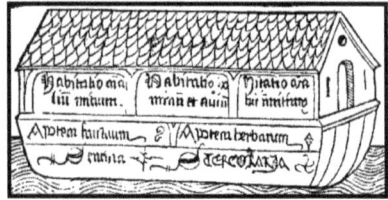

[1] *And I saw a new heaven and a new earth: for the first heaven and the first earth were passed away; and there was no more sea*

[2] *And I John saw the holy city, new Jerusalem, coming down from God out of heaven, prepared as a bride adorned for her husband.*   Revelation 21:1-2

The New Jerusalem will descend from heaven and man will spend eternity living in the new world (Revelation 21-22).

7.0 The Ark had Many Rooms

It has been estimated that there were over 6000 different species of animals in the ark of varying sizes. There must have been a lot of rooms spread over the three levels of the ark. The total available floor space on the Ark would have been over 100,000 square feet, which would be more floor space than 20 standard-sized basketball courts. Assuming an 18-inch cubit, Noah's Ark would have had a cubic volume equal to 570 modern railroad stock cars. The total cubic volume would have been 1,518,000 cubic feet. When Jesus Christ met with His disciples a short time before He was nailed to the Cross of Calvary, He spoke of a place that He would prepare for them and all who would believe upon His name.

In my Father's house are many mansions: if it were not so, I would have told you. I go to prepare a place for you
        John 14:2

It is interesting that Joseph the father of Jesus was a carpenter, and It is certain that Jesus learned the trade as a young child and teenager. Jesus Christ stated that He was going before all of those who would follow to prepare a place for them. While not specifically stated in the scriptures who built it, the New Jerusalem is a city that will house all the Old and New Testament saints (Revelation 21:2). The city is very large, being a cube that is about 1500 miles long, wide and high. The saints will go in and out of the New Jerusalem forever, and there will be no light for the Lord God giveth them light: and they shall reign forever and ever (Revelation 22:5).

8.0 The Ark Carried Beasts Good and Bad

The ark was loaded with every species of animals and birds. There was no discrimination between those that might be considered good or bad creatures. The Kingdom of heaven will be like the ark, it will be given to those who have received Jesus Christ as their Lord and Savior regardless of how much sin was in every person's life. There will be pastors, evangelists prostitutes and murderers who will inherit the kingdom of heaven. The blood of Jesus Christ is sufficient to save all, just as the ark was sufficient to save Noah, his family, and a remnant of every creature that walked upon the earth.

[3] *For we ourselves also were sometimes foolish, disobedient, deceived, serving divers lusts and pleasures, living in malice and envy, hateful, and hating one another.*

[4] *But after that the kindness and love of God our Saviour toward man appeared,*

[5] *Not by works of righteousness which we have done, but according to his mercy he saved us, by the washing of regeneration, and renewing of the Holy Ghost;*

[6] *Which he shed on us abundantly through Jesus Christ our Saviour;*

[7] *That being justified by his grace, we should be made heirs according to the hope of eternal life*   Titus 3:3-7

So the last shall be first, and the first last: for many be called,
but few chosen   Matthew 20:16

One of the fascinating things that was
discovered as this book was being written is
the fact that a *unicorn* actually existed
before the flood! It will be surprise to many,
but the unicorn was actually mentioned in
the bible on 8 different occasions (Job 39: 9-
10 for example). There is a song that was made popular by the
Irish Rovers.

<blockquote>

Noah looked out through the driving rain
and the unicorns were hiding, playing silly games
They were kicking and splashing while the rain was
pourin'
Oh those silly unicorns!
The ark started moving, and it drifted with the tide
and the unicorns looked up from the rocks and they
cried
And the waters came down and just floated them away,
That's why you never see a unicorn to this very
day....

</blockquote>

Eternal life and the kingdom of heaven is offered freely to all.
Salvation is by faith and grace to all who would believe upon the
Lord Jesus Christ. Salvation is offered free, but it is only
appropriated to those who will believe in faith. Like the
unicorns, there will be those who will not want to Go into the
ark; which is Jesus Christ. They will die in rebellion according to
their own choice and it will be too late. Have you accepted
Christ as your Lord and savior and became a part of the body of
Christ? If not, do it today before the "ark" leaves forever.

115

9.0 The Ark Had no Rudder

When Noah and his family built the ark, there is no mention of a rudder. Everyone who has set out upon the water in a boat knows that that every vessel must have a rudder. Without a rudder to steer the boat, it simply moves aimlessly upon the water. Life on this earth is exactly like the ark. When Jesus Christ died upon the Cross of Calvary he left this world to be with His Father in Heaven. His disciples and followers were devastated: *What will we do without our Lord and Savior they cried?* When Christ died and ascended into heaven He knew that man needed divine guidance, and so He sent the promise of the Holy Spirit to dwell within all true believers. The Holy spirit will *guide you in all things*, it is the *great comforter* and it will guide every Christian through the swamps of life. Without the Holy Spirit to guide you in all things, your boat (your body) has no way to discern right from wrong and rebuke sin. It is not difficult to understand why the world is full of murders, abusers, rapists and decidedly wicked people. Without the Holy Spirit there is no moral compass , no purpose and no direction. Those who do not have the gift of the Holy Spirit have no moral compass.

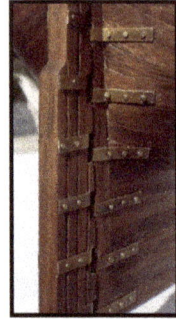

Raging waves of the sea, foaming out their own shame; wandering stars, to whom is reserved the blackness of darkness forever Jude 1:13

10.0 The Ark Had No Power of Its Own

The ark was tossed and turned upon the waves with no form of power. Any sailor will tell you that his worst fear is to lose engine power during a storm. The ark rose up from where it was built, and Noah had no idea where he and his cargo were going. As previously discussed, the ark moved across the waters for over 600 miles, and on the 17th day of the 7th month it rested over the Mountains of Ararat. This was exactly where God wanted the ark, and that was exactly where it stayed. As Christians, we have no righteousness of our own. All that we have is the saving grace of our Lord Jesus Christ. Those who have been called by God have been given the authority to heal the sick, peach the gospel message and to defeat Satan. This power is sustained and guaranteed by the Gift of the Holy Spirit, who dwells within all born again believers. Some teach that the apostolic ministry that healed the sick, raised the dead and cast out demons was only for that time and place. Nothing could be farther than the truth. When Christ died for our sins, the veil that separated man from God was rent in two, opening the way to communion with God the Father. All power and authority comes from God and is exercised by faith. In Jesus Christ the born-again Christian now has access (spiritually) to the very throne of God, where Christ is always seated at the right hand of God the Father interceding for us. This is not mere speculation, Jesus Christ himself said:

[12] *Verily, verily, I say unto you, He that believeth on me, the works that I do shall he do also; and greater works than these shall he do; because I go unto my Father.*

[13] *And whatsoever ye shall ask in my name, that will I do, that*

117

the Father may be glorified in the Son.
[14] *If ye shall ask any thing in my name, I will do it*
John 14:12-14

Christ said that He did nothing unless the Father told Him to do it (John 5:19, 6:38, 8:28). It is important for every Christian to clearly understand how the delegation of authority and power is administered by the Father. A biblical example of delegated authority and power is found in a son who comes of age. The son is given a *signet ring* by the father, and with this ring he is empowered to fully represent the affairs of the father. When the son spoke, the father spoke; when the son made a decision, it was guaranteed by the father. When Jesus was sent by the Father, he was sent with power and authority (John 5:22, Matthew 11:27. When Jesus chose His disciples, He empowered them to preach the gospel message with authority and power. He anointed them with the ability to cast out demons, heal the sick and cast out devils in His name. Today, all born-again Christians have been delegated the same power and authority; the apostolic gifts were not given only to His disciples during His earthly ministry, but to every Christian today. The seal and guarantee of this authority and power was the indwelling of the Holy Spirit. Today, the elect of God are also sent with the same authority and power and indwelled by the same Holy Spirit. There is no power within us unless it has been given by the Father through His Son Jesus Christ. These powers are manifested and made evident by the gifts of the Holy Spirit.

[1] *And there shall come forth a rod out of the stem of Jesse, and a Branch shall grow out of his roots:*
[2] *And the spirit of the LORD shall rest upon him, the spirit of*

118

wisdom and understanding, the spirit of counsel and might, the spirit of knowledge and of the fear of the LORD   Isaiah 11:1-2

11.0 God Commanded Noah to Build an Ark Out of Gopher Wood

No one knows where gopher wood came from and where it went. Jesus Christ is the Son of God. He was not chosen by a hereditary line or social position like the Levitical priesthood, but He is of the order of Melchisedec. He has no beginning and He has no end. He was the son of God before the creation of the world, and all things were made by and through Him. God the Father spoke the words that brought the universe into existence, but Jesus Christ the Son was the agent who brought these things to pass. The Bible says of Jesus:

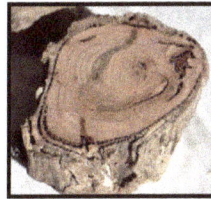

[1] *In the beginning was the Word, and the Word was with God, and the Word was God.*
[2] *The same was in the beginning with God.*
[3] *All things were made by him; and without him was not anything made that was made*   John 1:1-3

12.0 The Ark Contained Everything that Noah and His Family Needed

Jesus Christ is sufficient to sustain us and to meet *all* of our needs.

But my God shall supply all your needs according to his riches in glory by Christ Jesus   Philippians 4:19

His divine power hath given unto us all things that pertain unto life and godliness, through the knowledge of him that hath called us to glory and virtue II Peter 1:3

Having the Lord Jesus Christ is to have everything needed in both this life and the life to come. To have Him is to have everything. Not to have Him is to have absolutely nothing at all. All joy, peace, meaning, value, purpose, hope, fulfillment in life now and forever is bound up in Christ. And when a person receives Jesus Christ as Lord and Savior, they enter in to an all-sufficient relationship with an all-sufficient Christ.

13.0 Everyone Who was Saved by Noah's Ark Was Saved by Faith

Noah was told 120 years before the flood that judgment was coming upon sinful man. Since every person has sinned and fallen short of the glory of God, this must have scared both Noah and his family. How would they escape God's wrath? The answer is the same today as it was then; by faith. Noah and his family believed that if they trusted God that they would be saved. Salvation and eternal life is promised to every person, Jew or Gentile, who would believe upon His name. To have faith in Jesus Christ means to trust Him...completely....Without reservation....and to believe that He is the only Son of the Living God. Salvation and eternal life is freely offered to anyone who will accept it by simple faith. So it was in the days of Noah. We can be sure that Noah warned the people to repent and be saved, but only he and his family believed in Gods saving grace. It is the same today; *many are called but few will respond*.

14.0 The Flood Came Suddenly

Everyone had been warned for 120 years, but the flood came suddenly. Once Noah and his family were safely in the ark, God himself sealed them inside the ark and they were all saved.

By faith Noah, being warned of God of things not seen as yet, moved with fear, prepared an ark to the saving of his house; by the which he condemned the world, and became heir of the righteousness which is by faith   Hebrews 11:7

Once anyone has accepted Jesus Christ as their personal Lord and Savior, they are saved and sealed with the Holy Spirit. Noah and his family were saved from the moment that they believed God's word. Jesus Christ is coming again soon, and it will be suddenly and without warning. We have also been warned of His 2^{cd} coming and have been waiting almost 2000 years. However, there will be many who will have no idea what is happening, and many Christians who will be totally surprised. Just as it was in the days of Noah, so it will be when Jesus returns again.

[27] *They did eat, they drank, they married wives, they were given in marriage, until the day that Noe entered into the ark, and the flood came, and destroyed them all.*
[28] *Likewise also as it was in the days of Lot; they did eat, they drank, they bought, they sold, they planted, they builded*   Luke 17:27-28

Luke 17:27-28 have often been misinterpreted. There is nothing wrong with eating, marrying, buying things and building. The message is that people will not be anticipating and hoping that Christ will take them up to heaven and be with Him forever. Many will refuse to believe that Jesus Christ is coming again soon. People will not be serving Christ and praising Him daily, but they will be more interested in routine activities than serving Jesus Christ. Christ has warned us that when He returns to rapture out the saints, just as in the days of Noah, many will be unprepared for His return. It will be a sad day when there is no Christian left on earth to fight against Satan and His forces.

[3] *But if our gospel be hid, it is hid to them that are lost:*
[4] *In whom the god of this world hath blinded the minds of them which believe not, lest the light of the glorious gospel of Christ, who is the image of God, should shine unto them* II Corinthians 4:3-4

15.0 Noah was Saved, but Did Not Just Ride Along

Once Noah and his family entered the ark, they could not just hang in a hammock all day and wait for their deliverance. There was much work to be done, and there were many things that had to be taken care of on a daily basis. As born-again Christians, we are not just supposed to accept Christ as our Lord and Savior and then never serve Him. It is certainly true that once a person has accepted Christ as their savior that salvation is a free gift:

[8] *For by grace are ye saved through faith; and that not of yourselves: it is the gift of God:*
[9] *Not of works, lest any man should boast* Ephesians 2:8-9

We cannot work our way to heaven, but because we have been redeemed by the blood of the Lamb, we *will* have good works ; not to *be saved* but because we *are saved* not by works but by the Grace of God. However, if any person truly accepts Christ as their Lord and Savior, that person will have good works.

[21] *Was not Abraham our father justified by works, when he had offered Isaac his son upon the altar?*
[22] *Seest thou how faith wrought with his works, and by works was faith made perfect?*
[23] *And the scripture was fulfilled which saith, Abraham believed God, and it was imputed unto him for righteousness: and he was called the Friend of God.*
[24] *Ye see then how that by works a man is justified, and not by faith only.*
[25] *Likewise also was not Rahab the harlot justified by works, when she had received the messengers, and had sent them out another way?*
[26] *For as the body without the spirit is dead, so **faith without works is dead** also*   Romans 2: 21-26

Once a person is truly born again and accepts Jesus Christ as their Lord and savior, Jesus Christ is living and dwelling in our hearts. Because of Christ and the gif of the Holy Spirit, we become *new creatures in Christ*. We are living temporarily in this world, but we are not of this world. We cannot help but have good works in our lives; doing good for other; helping those less fortunate than ourselves and proclaiming the *good news* of the *gospel message*. That sold-out, sincere Christian will *want* to glorify our Father which is in heaven. That is true Christianity. If we are doing good for others so that we will bring glory to ourselves, then we have the wrong motive. if We think

123

that any amount of work will justify us before God, the works which we perform are like wood, hay and stubble.

[12] *Now if any man build upon this foundation gold, silver, precious stones, wood, hay, stubble;*

[13] *Every man's work shall be made manifest: for the day shall declare it, because it shall be revealed by fire; and the fire shall try every man's work of what sort it is.*

[14] *If any man's work abide which he hath built thereupon, he shall receive a reward.*

[15] *If any man's work shall be burned, he shall suffer loss: but he himself shall be saved; yet so as by fire.*

[16] *Know ye not that ye are the temple of God, and that the Spirit of God dwelleth in you?*
Corinthians 3: 12-16

[17] *Even so faith, if it hath not works, is dead, being alone.*

[18] *Yea, a man may say, Thou hast faith, and I have works: shew me thy faith without thy works, and I will shew thee my faith by my works* James 2:17-18

So, faith without works is dead. If we have faith, we will have works. Our works will not save us, because we are saved by grace. But our works will be judged and rewarded. Our rewards for our works done in love and faith will be at the *Bema Seat Judgment* after the rapture of the saints.

And I saw the dead, small and great, stand before God; and the books were opened: and another book was opened, which is the book of life: and the dead were judged out of those things which were written in the books Revelation 20:12

16.0 Noah and His Family Were Totally Dependent Upon God for Their Salvation

When God called out Noah, he was told to build an Ark. Noah no doubt replied; *build what?* God gave Noah detailed plans to build a gigantic boat.

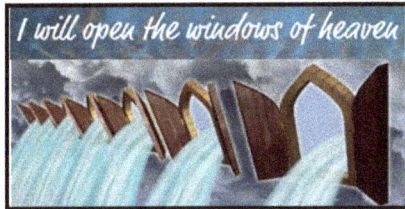

I will open the windows of heaven

Would it float? Where would it take them? What would they eat? Noah was told to load 2 of every unclean animal and 3 of every clean animal...Bears, lions, wolves??....*Are you kidding me Lord* ? Noah must have had boundless faith. He was totally dependent upon God to tell him what to do and how to do it. He was totally dependent upon God to save him and his family when every other human on earth perished.

Those who accept Jesus Christ as their Lord and Savior must have exactly the same kind of faith.

For we are saved by hope: but hope that is seen is not hope: for what a man seeth, why doth he yet hope for?   Romans 8:24

[1] *Now faith is the substance of things hoped for, the evidence of things not seen.*

[3] *Through faith we understand that the worlds were framed by the word of God, so that things which are seen were not made of things which do appear.*

[7] *By faith Noah, being warned of God of things not seen as yet, moved with fear, prepared an ark to the saving of*

*his house; by the which he condemned the world, and
became heir of the righteousness which is by faith.*

[13] *These all died in faith, not having received the promises,
but having seen them afar off, and were persuaded
of them, and embraced them, and confessed that they
were strangers and pilgrims on the earth*
Hebrews 11: 1,3,7,13

There is no Christian today who has ever seen Christ. There is no
proof that Christ rose from the dead. There is no proof that
either heaven or eternal life exists. Each Christian walks in faith.

*I am crucified with Christ: nevertheless I live; yet not I, but Christ
liveth in me: and the life which I now live in the flesh I live by
the faith of the Son of God, who loved me, and gave himself for
me* Galatians 2:20

17.0 Noah and His Family Were Rebuked and Ridiculed for Building the Ark

Imagine the social rejection that Noah
and his family must have experienced
while they were building the ark. For an
unknown period of time, Noah would
have spent each day gathering the wood
have spent each day gathering the wood
needed and building the ark piece by piece, board by board.
People would have ridiculed Noah and his sons and called then
crazy. Noah would have warned the people of the wrath to
come but they would not have listened to him. He was leaving a
wicked and evil world and the world rejected him.

So it is for all Christians today. Those who sincerely and by faith choose to accept Jesus Christ as their Lord and Savior will be at enmity with this world. Christ warned that Christians will not be a part of this world, although they are in the world.

[18] *If the world hate you, ye know that it hated me before it hated you.*
[19] *If ye were of the world, the world would love his own: but because ye are not of the world, but I have chosen you out of the world, therefore the world hateth you*
John 15:18-19

The Pharisees and the Sadducees, the ruling class of the Jews, hated Jesus because he was a threat to their social status and condemned them for misinterpreting the law of Moses. They were constantly trying to harass Him and kill Him. People who live in the world today will also seek to persecute or at least ridicule the Christian way of life. It is not necessarily the lack of inherent character and morality in those who ridicule, but the presence and influence of Satan in their lives. They have no moral compass to lead them, and without the Holy Spirit to guide them they turn to sin and rebellion against all holy things. Just as in Noah's day, the Christian who wars against Satan and his demonic forces will never be accepted by a sinful and lost world. The non-Christian has no life to look forward to except for the present life, and without the grace of Jesus Christ they have no hope for life after death. They cannot find the real peace and abiding love that Jesus Christ has to offer, so they reject those who have found those pearls. They are like ships without a rudder; leaves blowing in the wind; and tossed and turned by every wave upon a sea of unrest.

127

[2] *For men shall be lovers of their own selves, covetous,*
boasters, proud, blasphemers, disobedient to parents,
unthankful, unholy,

[3] ***Without natural affection,*** *trucebreakers, false accusers,*
incontinent, fierce, despisers of those that are good,

[4] *Traitors, heady, highminded,* ***lovers of pleasures*** *more than*
lovers of God;

[5] *Having a form of godliness, but denying the power thereof:*
from such turn away.

[6] *For of this sort are they which creep into houses, and lead*
captive silly women laden with sins, led away with
divers lusts,

[7] *Ever learning, and never able to come to the knowledge of*
the truth   II Timothy 2:3-7

From such things, ***turn away.***

18.0 Noah and His family Had No Idea Where God Was Leading Them

When the great flood came upon the earth, the ark rose above the earth and began to move. It was more than one year later before the ark came to rest. During this period of time, Noah and his family had no idea where God was taking them. In simple faith, they all waited shut up inside the ark. Finally, the ark rested upon the Mountains of Ararat. When the door was finally opened, Noah emerged to a place that he had never seen before. Nevertheless, Noah emerged from the ark confident that God had called them to that place and that He was sufficient to see them through.

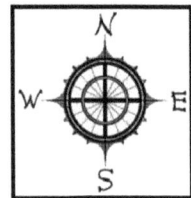

128

Those who have accepted Jesus Christ as their redeemer and savior leave a place that they have become familiar with and are a new creature born-again into God's kingdom. They are in the world but never a part of the world.

Therefore if any man be in Christ, he is a new creature: old things are passed away; behold, all things are become new
    II Corinthians 5:17

When anyone accepts Jesus Christ as their Lord and Savior they are no longer the *old man* but become a **new man** and become a part of the body of Jesus Christ. The experience of accepting Christ is a new journey through life. The phrase *born again* literally means *born from above*. The act of being "born again" carries the idea of becoming *a child of God.* This new *spiritual birth* is compared to a child who enters the world through a natural birth. Christ wants a born-again Christian to put all of their faith in Him, and be dependent upon Him for all things. Just as a new-born babe must grow up and learn how to think and act, the new Christian must also grow up and become mature in Jesus Christ. Each new Christian receives the gift of the Holy Spirit, who will guide him/her in all things. The new Christian will be led into a new lifestyle with new gifts from the Holy Spirit. One must trust God and accept the responsibility to function and operate in the Gifts as Christ chooses. Like Noah and his family, it is usually not known where this new life will lead a new Christian. One must be patient and respond as called. The journey will lead one to new friends, new thoughts and new responsibilities. The moment you believe in Jesus Christ, there is a spiritual metamorphosis and everything changes! One now lives by faith and not by sight: *For sin shall not have dominion over you: for ye are not under the law, but* *under grace* (Romans 6:14). A true life, a better life, a wonderful life is only found in Jesus Christ. When you become a Christian, you have new life in him.

The Mystery of the 17th Day of the 7th Month

In Genesis 17:11 it was revealed that the ark rested upon the mountains of Ararat in the seventh month, on the seventeenth day of the month. Noah and the ark were not resting upon solid ground as we discussed in Chapter 2, but they rested and became stationary over the place that God had chosen. This fact is not important to the flood narrative, and in fact has created much mystery and confusion in the flood narrative. Why was this fact inserted into the flood account? There is prophetic significance in this one event. There is a remarkable set of Biblical events which occurred on the 17th day of the 7th month.

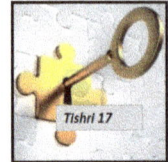

- **The Exodus From Egypt**

Hundreds of years later, God was moved to rescue the Children of Israel from slaver and servitude in Egypt. God had again raised up a man who would faithfully serve Him; that person was Moses whom God had miraculously saved 80 years before by placing him as an infant in an ark, which was also sealed with pitch and also floated upon the waters of the Nile River. Moses was called at age 80 to speak to the Pharaoh of Egypt and persuade him to let the Children of Israel go. After bringing 9 plagues upon Egypt, the Pharaoh refused to liberate the people. Finally, God had tolerated the Pharaoh enough. He

130

decided to kill all of the firstborn of Egypt using His death angel as the instrument of death.

To protect the Children of Israel from the death angel, a perfect Lamb of one year lamb was slaughtered on the afternoon of Wednesday, Nisan 14. The blood of the lamb was collected, and smeared over the entrance (lintel) of the house with a hyssop brush. The Lamb was to be eaten that evening (Nisan 15) and the people would wait for the death angel to Passover the house. The Blood of the Lamb would protect them. At midnight as each family sat by the fire, the Death angel killed the firstborn of every family and animal in Egypt. One child was the Son of the Pharaoh. In despair, he finally told the Children of Israel to *go, leave*. To commemorate their exodus from Egypt, God instituted the Feast of Passover on Nisan 14 and the Feast of Unleavened Bread which began on Nisan 17 and ended on Nisan23. Now the surprise! God also instituted the Feast of Firstfruits, which began on the day following the only Sabbath (Saturday), which was that year on Sunday, Nisan 17. Jesus Christ was crucified on Nisan 14 and 3 days later He rose from the grave on Nisan 17 !! But that is not all.

Israel came through the Red Sea on the 17th of Nisan having left on the first day of Unleavened Bread. For them this was death to their old life (with the drowning of the Egyptians) and resurrection to a new life in God on the 17th!

- ***The Manna in The Wilderness***

God had provided food for everything in the ark during the great flood. God provided *manna* (what is it?) as food for the Children of Israel during the 40 years

131

they wandered in the wilderness. The manna which had fed the nation of Israel for 40 years in the wilderness stopped when Joshua crossed the River Jordan on the 16th of Nisan and from Nisan 17 onwards Israel feasted on the new grain of the promised land (Josh 5:10-12).

- **Haman Seeks to Destroy Israel**

A death sentence hung over the entire nation of Israelite when Haman conspired with the King to sign a decree to destroy every Israelite (Esther 3:1-12). The decree went out on the 13th of Nisan (Esther 3:12). Esther then proclaimed a three day fast (Esther 4:16) for the 14th, 15th and 16th. On the 3rd day (Esther 5:1) Esther approached the king in an effort to save Israel. She placed her faith in God and declared: *If I perish, I perish...It is in God's hands!* On the 17th of Nisan, Haman was caught in a divine trap and instead of the Jews being destroyed, his own life was taken!

- **Hezekiah Cleanses the Temple**

Upon becoming king, Hezekiah found the Temple of the Lord had fallen into a state of disrepair and desecration. He immediately commenced a great religious reform. In eight days they had re-opened the great Temple of Solomon and cleansed it of all defilement (2 Chronicles 29:1-17). The cleansing of the temple was not completed until the sixteenth day of the first month (Nisan). The temple resumed service on the next day, Nisan 17.

- **Jesus Christ is Crucified**

Our Lord Jesus Christ was crucified on
the afternoon of Nisan 14, at the same
time that the first Passover lamb was
slain over 1500 years earlier. Christ lay in
the grave for three full days and three
full nights. He rose from the grave after 3
days and 3 nights on the 1^{sd} day of Feast of Firstfruits, which fell
on Nisan 17 in 30 AD !!

Christ was the *firstfruit* of all who would believe upon His
promises and be resurrected from the dead or raptured at His
2nd coming (I Corinthians 15: 20-23).

The Four Arks

There are 3 arks which are important in the scriptural records:
(1) Noah's ark (2) The ark of Moses (3) The ark of the covenant.
All were rectangular structures made of wood.

- *Noah's ark*

Noah's ark was made of a
mysterious wood called *gopher
wood*. it was sealed both out and in
by a *pitch*.

*Make thee an ark of gopher wood; rooms shalt thou make in the
ark, and shalt pitch it within and without with pitch*
        Genesis 6:14

The exact meaning of the term *gopher wood* is a hotly debated
topic. The Hebrew word translated as gopher is *kopher* which

133

simply means *to cover*. It has been translated as cypress, pine or cedar in several different versions of the Bible. The exact meaning of gopher wood is lost in antiquity, and any identification is purely speculation. It should be noted that the ark was built or constructed of something called gopher wood, and this is not to be confused with the word *pitch* which was applied both inside and out to make it waterproof. Skeptics have said that pitch is derived from petroleum products and that the biblical account is wrong, claiming that this process was not known until much later. They fail to recognize that God supervised building of the ark, and that the production of pitch from a petroleum base could have been fully revealed to Noah. However, there is a 2^{cd} well-known source of pitch and that is from the sap of coniferous trees such as a pine tree. It is a historical fact that the production of pitch from tree sap was known and used in antiquity. Later, both the Greeks and Romans sealed their wooden vessels with pitch from trees. Whether Noah was told by God how to produce such pitch, or whether it was known at that time, is pure speculation.

- ***The Ark of Moses***

The ark of Moses was tiny compared to the ark of Noah. It was built to save the baby Moses from the destruction of all male Hebrew children (Exodus 1:22).

[1] *And there went a man of the house of Levi, and took to wife a daughter of Levi.*
[2] *And the woman conceived, and bare a son: and when she saw him that he was a goodly child, she hid him three months.*

[3] *And when she could not longer hide him, she took for him an ark of bulrushes, and daubed it with slime and with pitch, and put the child therein; and she laid it in the flags by the river's brink* Exodus 2:1-3

The Hebrew word for ark is only used in describing Noah's ark and Moses' ark (*Kopher*). Noah's ark was made of Gopher wood, but the ark of Moses was made of *bulrushes*. The Hebrew word translated as bulrush is *gome*. Gome was likely the brushy stalks of bulrush, which grew in great quantities by the Nile River. The ark was sealed with *slime* and *pitch*. The slime which covered the ark was likely thick, dried mud from the banks of the Nile. The word *pitch* in Exodus 2:3 is derived from the same root word used in Genesis 6:14. We do not know the dimensions of Moses' infant ark, but we can assume that it was similar to a pointed, rectangular shaped boat that would hold a small baby. We also know that it had a *cover* because when Pharaoh's daughter found this ark floating in the river, she *opened it* in order to see the child (Exodus 2:5-6).

- **The Ark of the Covenant**

The third ark was made of what was called *shittim wood* and was built by Moses at Mt. Sinai using instructions directly issued by the Lord. The Ark of the Covenant was the most important piece of furniture in the tabernacle. It stood in the tabernacle inside an enclosure called the *Holy of Holies*. It was not to be seen by ordinary men, but only by the High Priest; and that only once a year on the *Feast of Atonement*. The High Priest would first offer a sin sacrifice for himself, wash himself

ritually clean, and then he would sprinkle blood on the Alter of Incense which stood in the Holy Place. He would then pass through the veil which separated the Holy Place from the Holy of Holies, sprinkle the blood of the sacrifice upon the four horns of the covering of the ark, and then plead for the sins of the people.

It is interesting that Moses was intimately involved in both his own ark as a babe and as the construction foreman for the holy ark of the covenant (Exodus 25:10-16).The ark of the covenant, just like Noah's ark, was shaped like a rectangular box. It's dimensions in cubits were 2 1/2 long by 1 1/2 wide by 1 1/2 high. That is approximately 3 feet and 9 inches long and 2 feet and 3 inches wide and high. It was actually quite small. It also had a lid or a covering on it. This covering is called the *mercy seat* (Exodus 26:34). The ark of the covenant was hollow inside and later held various items which God commanded to be placed there; the golden pot that had manna, Aaron's rod that budded, and the tables of the 10 commandments (Heb. 9:4).

By the time that King Solomon moved the Holy Ark to the newly built Temple, it only contained the two tables of stone on which Moses had written the Ten Commandments (1 Kings 8:9). Where the pot of manna and the rod of Aaron went, nobody knows. The ark of the covenant was a special symbol of God's presence. God promised Moses that *there I will meet with thee, and I will commune with thee from above the mercy seat* (Exodus 25:22). The presence of the Lord and the Ark of the Covenant disappeared when the Southern Kingdom of Israel was conquered and deported for 70 years by the Babylonians in 586 BC. Where the ark went and where it is now is a matter of speculation. Some say that it was hidden in a cave by Ezekiel;

some say it was taken to Ethiopia; and others say it remains hidden in the subterranean passages beneath the Dome of the Rock. Jewish tradition holds that when their long-awaited Messiah arises to redeem all Israel, that the ark of the covenant will be found and placed again in a new temple.

- **The Spiritual Ark: Jesus Christ**

The ark that Noah built is more than just an interesting story, it is a powerful type of Jesus Christ. We have pointed out eighteen examples of how the ark foreshadowed the person and works of Jesus. The ark of Noah is a picture and type of salvation. It represents deliverance from the wrath of God. The ark of Moses is a picture of God's love and protection. The ark of the covenant is a picture of God's mercy and grace. All are prophetic pictures of how God would send His only begotten Son to earth to forgive our sins, and offer salvation and eternal life to all who would believe upon His holy name. Each person must trust in the ark of Jesus Christ at some time in their life to obtain eternal salvation. If anyone is to achieve peace and hope upon this earth and eternal life in the world to come they must put their faith in Jesus Christ. There is no other way to achieve salvation, deliverance and mercy except to believe upon His Holy name and confess that He is the Son of God. He and He alone is the ark of our salvation. Just as Noah was within the ark we must be within Him. A day is coming when the door to the ark will be closed. In John 10 Jesus said:

I am the Door, if anyone enters through Me, he will be saved, and will go in and out and find pasture John 10:9

137

Strive to enter in at the strait gate: for many, I say unto you, will seek to enter in, and shall not be able Luke 13:24

But there will be a day when it will be too late to enter into His kingdom: The door will be closed.

When once the master of the house is risen up, and hath shut the door, and ye begin to stand without, and to knock at the door, saying, Lord, Lord, open unto us; and he shall answer and say unto you, I know you not whence ye are: Luke 13:25

A day is coming when the door to His eternal ark will not open. Saints, delay no longer....Get on board the ark, both you and your entire family.

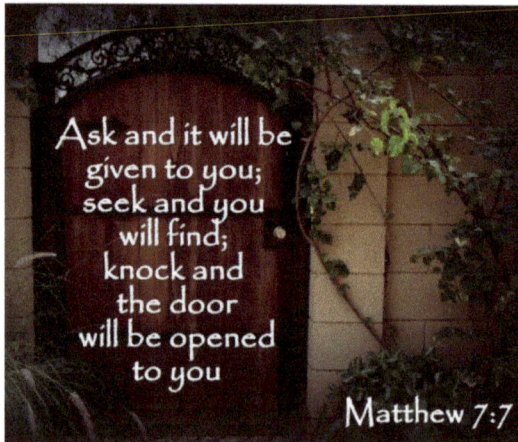

Ask and it will be given to you; seek and you will find; knock and the door will be opened to you
Matthew 7:7

Bibliography

Other Books by Don T. Phillips

- The Book of Revelation: *Mysteries Revealed*

- The Book of Exodus: *Historical and Prophetic Truths*

- The Birth and Death of Christ

- A Biblical Chronology from Adam to Christ

- A Sequential Chronology of End Time Events

- A Sequential Chronology of End Time Events: *Expanded Edition*

- The Book of Ruth: *Historical and Prophetic Truths*

- Dispensations, Covenants and The Eternal Plan of God

- Life After Death: *Mysteries Revealed*

All are available from:

Virtualbookworm Publishing Company, PO Box 9949, College Station Texas, 77842
www.virtualbookworm.com

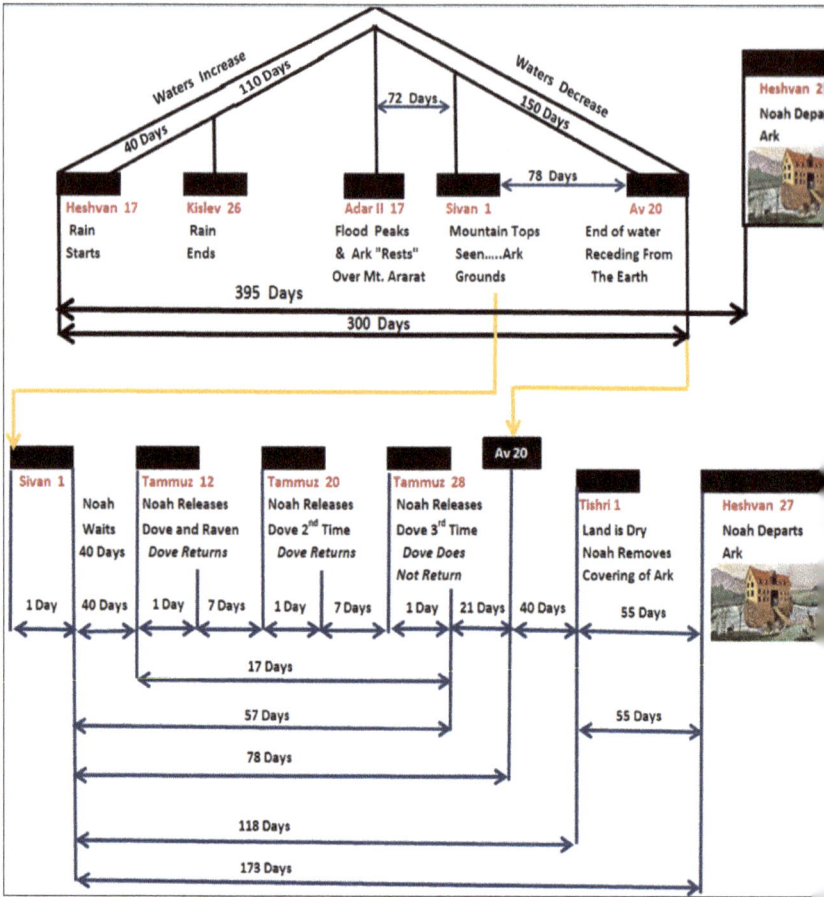

Waters Increase

40 Days · 110 Days · 72 Days

Waters Decrease

150 Days · 78 Days

Heshvan 17	Kislev 26	Adar II 17	Sivan 1	Av 20
Rain Starts	Rain Ends	Flood Peaks & Ark "Rests" Over Mt. Ararat	Mountain Tops Seen.....Ark Grounds	End of water Receding From The Earth

395 Days

300 Days

Heshvan 2
Noah Depa[rts]
Ark

Sivan 1		Tammuz 12		Tammuz 20		Tammuz 28		Av 20	Tishri 1	Heshvan 27
	Noah Waits 40 Days	Noah Releases Dove and Raven *Dove Returns*		Noah Releases Dove 2nd Time *Dove Returns*		Noah Releases Dove 3rd Time *Dove Does Not Return*			Land is Dry Noah Removes Covering of Ark	Noah Departs Ark
1 Day	40 Days	1 Day	7 Days	1 Day	7 Days	1 Day	21 Days	40 Days	55 Days	

17 Days

57 Days

78 Days

55 Days

118 Days

173 Days

140

www.ingramcontent.com/pod-product-compliance
Lightning Source LLC
Chambersburg PA
CBHW040421110426

42813CB00014B/2728